THE PRINCE OF PEACE

THE PRINCE OF PEACE

Finding true peace in a world that wars ....

Peter Sammons

Glory to Glory Publications

First published in Great Britain by
Glory to Glory Publications
an imprint of
Buy Research Ltd

Glory to Glory Publications
PO Box 212 SAFFRON WALDEN CB10 2UU

www.glorytoglory.co.uk

ISBN 978-0-9926674-3-6

Printed in Great Britain by Imprint Digital, Exeter

CONTENTS

INTRODUCTION

Peace....

If there's one thing this world seems to desire it is peace, that ability to live life without fear of warfare or harm. Peace, of course, is more than just an absence of war. We can have un-peaceful neighbourhoods and un-peaceful families. Saddest of all, perhaps, we can have un-peaceful individuals, picking quarrels with their neighbours, or struggling with guilt or shame or with the effects of individual persecution, unable to be at peace with themselves. Is this life at its best? Was it all meant to be this way? Can life be better than it is? And what are the prospects for the future? We will explore these questions throughout this book.

For whom is this book written? What sort of readers does the author anticipate might want to explore this subject? We might think that everyone would have a practical interest in peace – that everyone might be considered a stakeholder (to use a decidedly modern term) in the matter of peace. To look at the adventure films that emerge from Hollywood, Bollywood and all their emulators, it seems that peace is not a prime thought or theme for film makers or film-goers. If a film does not have explosions and absurd computer-generated "stunts" in the first five minutes, it is unlikely to hold the attention of a rising generation of viewers, for whom a disconnect between the real, and the supposedly more exciting imaginary, is growing ever wider. Computer games, at least for boys, also seem to focus on un-pacific themes where heroes are often anti-heroes and the young identify with the forces of disorder, not the upholders of law!

If we believe in God, generally speaking we believe that He is profoundly good and desires the best for the humans over which He is the only Deity. 'Is God *really* good?' has become a hotly debated question amongst some, but the debate is usually framed in the wrong terms of reference, as humans try to "judge" God by their own standards – and try to work out what they would "do" if they were God. In the book *The Empty Promise of Godism*[1] there is a useful chapter entitled "Is God Good?", which examines this question from a specifically biblical standpoint. Your author finds that God is indeed good, and encourages others to seek out a profoundly GOOD God for themselves.[2]

This book is about peace. What it is – and what it is not. How it might be found – and retained. This book casts light on what the Bible says about the future. Readers will find that this book is principally a Bible study, helping us to see what God has said about peace in its various and different guises. It is not a philosophical book, and nor does it try to anticipate every question a reader might have about peace. It is the Lord Jesus who is the ultimate realist about peace and war. In His teaching about the end of the world order as we know it, found in Matthew chapters 24 and 25, Jesus reminded His disciples as he reminds us that until the end **"You will hear of wars and rumours of wars, but see to it that you are not alarmed. Such things must happen, but the end is still to come"** (Matthew 24:6). If we speak about bringing an end to military conflicts in this world by our own efforts then we must ask ourselves, was Jesus wrong? Allowing that warfare will accompany mankind until the end, do we just shrug our shoulders and do nothing? Certainly not, because earlier Jesus had already said **"Blessed are the peacemakers, for they will be called children of God"** (Matthew 5:9).

---

[1] See bibliography

[2] *The Empty Promise of Godism* is available free online as PDF files chapter by chapter. Just Google Glory to Glory Publications. Information correct at August 2014.

There is a pressure group called *Christian Peacemaker Teams International* ("CPT") which originated in the USA and seems to have found its forte in opposing US foreign policy. CPT seeped into public consciousness in the West largely as a result of its team which blundered into the Iraq conflict zone in 2002, before the Iraq – Coalition war of 2003, apparently to use themselves as human shields in the event of a Coalition invasion. They remained after the war and were then abducted by the 'Swords of Righteousness Brigade' – one of the many militant sectarian groups in Baghdad that were causing appalling suffering on a purely sectarian basis. After three and a half months of negotiation and investigation, the CPT team were rescued by a team of international special forces, apparently led by the UK SAS (Special Air Service). Miraculously, no shot was fired. The CPT team were later criticised for their parsimonious "thanks" for their own rescue. Do we laud any and every stratagem aimed to "cause" peace, simply because it employs the term "Christian"? Were these 'peace-makers' actually advancing the cause of peace, or backing their own socio-cultural leanings? It is perhaps not for this author to pass judgement, but their view of 'peace' seems not entirely comfortable with what the Lord Jesus taught nor what the Bible records. Notably absent on their CPT website, when this author visited it, was any specific mention of God or His gospel – so the title "Christian" in their name may be more cultural than faith-based.

This book aims to explore what the Bible says about peace, and to major on what the Lord Jesus taught. What is greatly needed today is a rediscovery of what TRUE peace is, not a dewey-eyed sentimentality – a sort of 1960s "flower power" view of "peace", but a hard realistic look at what causes turmoil, what robs peace and what promotes evil. Most important of all, it explores how TRUE peace can be found and helps to set the scene on a future that Jesus tells us will not be peaceful – not in the way that the world at large understands that term. For Jesus' own disciples, He made one clear promise – one clear statement that shows us that 'peace' for us will not mean an absence of conflict nor a life of ease. Jesus said this:

John 15:18 **"If the world hates you, keep in mind that it hated me first"**. Following Jesus was never going to be easy – we are not called to a life of ease! Jesus also said:

Matthew 16:24 **"If anyone would come after me, let him deny himself and take up his cross and follow me. For whoever would save his life will lose it, but whoever loses his life for my sake will find it. For what will it profit a man if he gains the whole world and forfeits his soul? Or what shall a man give in return for his soul**?"

John 16:33 **"I have told you these things, so that in me you may have peace. In this world you will have trouble. But take heart! I have overcome the world."** (NIV).

True peace can be found. True peace can be possessed and lived-out. We need to have an appreciation of what the future holds. There are a growing band of "futurologists"[3] in the world today, but ironically it may well be that their (often expensive!) services are simply not needed, as the Bible actually gives clear clues as to what we can expect in the future. The task of men and women, no less boys and girls, is to prepare for that future and to be ready to meet it. But we can do this joyfully too, knowing that we have One Who has gone on ahead of us, and Who can give us that most profound peace which we desire in *this* world, as much as in *the next*. Not a life of ease – but a life of true peace. Now that's a life worth having!

Suffolk, England, October 2014

---

[3] People who guess what the future may hold, normally in return for a fee.

General Note – where readers see this symbol ⬚ offset to the right of the page, it is a suggestion that a specific Bible passage might be read. Readers can then track their progress by "ticking-off" or "checking-off" these symbols as they work through them.

Special Note – throughout this book we use the English word Jesus and its Hebrew counterpart *Yeshua* interchangeably. More and more Christians are using His Hebrew name in everyday discourse, so this seems entirely appropriate.

Chapter One

THINKING ABOUT PEACE

Setting the scene and some ground rules

We are embarked upon an exciting journey! Could there be anything more wonderful than the idea of peace? Is true peace possible? How can we obtain that true peace? And who is this *prince of peace* introduced in the Bible?

What is peace? What is the world's idea of peace? The Oxford English Dictionary gives us some clues:

> **Peace** = quiet, tranquillity, serenity
> (e.g. *peace of mind*). Freedom from or the cessation of war (e.g. *peace talks*).
> Freedom from civil disorder.
> **At Peace** = a state of friendliness.
> **Keep the peace** = prevent, or refrain from strife.
> **Peaceable** = disposed towards peace, un-warlike.

No doubt many people would be satisfied with these as basic definitions of peace and peacefulness. And most would probably say "give me a bit of that peace"! But the world we live in is not peaceable. At the time of writing this book, Russia is actively engaged in fighting in Ukraine. Simultaneously there are wars ongoing in Syria and Iraq with the real danger of spreading to other countries. There are civil disturbances and heavy State repression throughout the Middle East and Islamists are waging what they call *jihad* (holy war). Russia is cosying-up to China, selling advanced technology and difficult to obtain materials, to ease the effects of Western sanctions following Russia's belligerency in Ukraine, itself riven with communal tensions. Meantime China and the USA are trying to avoid an escalation of disagreement over freedom of navigation in the air and at sea. Japan and China are competitively re-arming. Weapons production and trading remains one of the staple industrial realities of commercial life. These (and other) international spats and potential spats and suspicions will continue. From time to time old enmities and old rivalries will erupt into open warfare – and many will die as a result. Resource wars – over energy, food and water – are now emerging as real threats to regional and global peace. Millions flee across borders each year to escape some of these harsh realities, if not the grinding poverty that robs them of true peace.

Un-peacefulness is not restricted to the level of international relations. Family breakdown is epidemic throughout the Western world, and possibly in the wider world. Marriage, if it is observed at all, can often amount to little more than *serial monogamy*, as one "partner" is swapped for another. Many children have no stable and settled family life. Slavery and virtual slavery is again becoming a reality after having been stamped-out by the Western powers in the nineteenth century. "Bride kidnap" and female genital mutilation are re-emerging as persistent social evils in many countries. Millions face disease and hunger – they do not enjoy 'peace'. In 2014 as this book is written, the appalling disease of Ebola is raging apparently unchecked and victims have nowhere to turn as medical facilities are overwhelmed. Others find their lives blighted by narcotic drugs. Many, especially Jews and Christians, face active persecution simply for being Jews or Christians. (Other religious minorities also face persecution – either State-sponsored or communal, but the most persistent persecution is undoubtedly reserved for Christians and Jews). We can say that all of this is "the world" going about its normal day to day business. That is life – as some would say!

If there is anything that we can say is common fare in this world, it is a lack of peace. The Bible is our point of reference in this book. It is the Bible that speaks of a *prince of peace* Whom mankind is to anticipate and welcome. The Bible also speaks of a time in the future – in this world – when there will be an unparalleled peace, ushered in by this Prince.

At this point some readers may encounter an immediate difficulty. They may not believe in the Bible and they may not believe in God. These difficulties do not mean you cannot read this book, but plainly they do place you at a considerable disadvantage! We simply invite you to hold on to your disbelief but to adopt a slightly different mindset – to allow for the possibility that God *does* exist and that the Bible continues to be His primary mechanism for speaking to people. True, the Bible tells us that God speaks in dreams, and that He speaks through events and situations, sometimes that He speaks in an audible way to individuals (your author has never yet had this experience, but otherwise level-headed people have claimed such experience). Sometimes God speaks *through* those who are followers of Jesus, through their words or their actions. But mostly God seems to speak through the pages of His Word – the Bible – and through His Word – Jesus, Whom Christians recognise as the Son of God (however politically incorrect that idea may be) and as Lord. In reading the Bible many people find an assurance that they are reading the "lively oracles"[1] of God – that God is actually speaking directly to them.

We offer no apology, then, for making the Bible the focus of this book. The Bible speaks of the past – although it is not primarily a history book. The Bible speaks much about the future – where a great deal of its focus lies. The Bible tells, overall, the story of Salvation – the story of peace. Naturally as the writer of *this* book, I encourage readers to

---

[1] In the Coronation event of Queen Elizabeth II in 1953, as the Bible was presented to the new Queen, the Archbishop of Canterbury declared "these are the lively oracles of God".

persist and to continue to read. If you come from a heavily "atheistic" background then you have two options – put down the book now and find another way to spend your next few evenings, or read on in the hope that you will get at least two worthwhile benefits. Firstly you will better understand the attitude of Jesus to peace and what He has said about the future. Secondly you may pick up some clues as to how to maximise your chances of finding a measure of peace *in this world* that may so far have eluded you. And that, dear reader, could be a wonderful thing!

The author recognises that most readers will approach this book with limited knowledge of the Bible – and some with absolutely no knowledge whatsoever. These readers can have confidence that in working through this book they will pick up a little 'head knowledge' along the way. This is not going to be a crash course on the Bible or on theology, but inevitably readers will pick up some understanding of the Bible as they follow the argument. In this introduction we will, however, make three simple observations about the Bible, so readers can get a clear sense of how the author approaches the subject:

* The Bible is divided into Old and New Testaments

This immediately sounds rather obscure and we acknowledge that these titles and divisions are not altogether helpful. The ***Old Testament*** tells of the dealings of God with humans in history, and especially through His chosen people – the Hebrews. The ***New Testament*** tells of God's dealings with humankind through Jesus, His Son, whom His followers called "Lord", as they acknowledged Him to be the ultimate authority over their lives. Old Testament and New Testament might better be thought of as "The Promise" (for the Old Testament) and "The Promise Fulfilled" for the New Testament. This at least recognises that the Old reveals God's quietly persistent promise that He will one day send a *prince of peace* to the world, whilst the New reveals who that *prince of peace* is. But even these titles are not altogether helpful, as some of the promises of the Old Testament (and indeed some promises in the New Testament) are yet to be fulfilled in the future. But, even so, try to hold on to the thought of *promise* and *promise fulfilled* as you work through this book. That idea at least provides a context in which to think about the 66 books that make up the Bible and the way the two "Testaments" stand in relation to each other. They are interconnected in very many ways – the New does not replace the Old – it confirms it. *Hand in glove* might be a better analogy for the way these two "Testaments" relate to each other.

* The Bible – is it dependable?

Let's just consider its dependability for a moment. In this book we do not set out to defend the Holy Scriptures as the definitive word of God. There are many useful books that examine the Holy Bible in that context and no doubt someone who is genuinely interested in this subject will readily find what they need without having to look too hard. If the reader comes to this book with the objection that the Bible *is not*, or *may not be*, the sole revelation of "god" then he or she is invited simply to "park" that objection for the time being. There surely can be no great problem in looking closely at what the Scriptures have to say about peace, so as to acquire a clear understanding of the argument being put forward in this book.

In a court of law, as each witness gives their testimony, a judge and jury will form an opinion as to the trustworthiness of that particular person, and the validity of the testimony they offer. The author invites the reader to adopt the same attitude towards the Bible. Readers can always "call more witnesses" at a later stage if they feel that the witness of Scripture is incomplete or invalid. The key suggestion made by this author is that a doubter holds on to his or her doubts but proceeds from this point onwards with the basic working assumption that the Scriptures *are* valid and trustworthy. If at the conclusion of this book the reader finds the testimony of

Scripture remains to them finally un-compelling, then he or she is free to take up their doubts once more. Until then, let us use the Scriptures as the platform from which to review what God says to us about this question of peace.

Allowing that many readers will be Westerners, then we might as well also "park" the gender issue: some may feel that reference to God as 'Him' and 'He' represents some form of gender aggression. If so, you too are simply invited to "park" that objection for the time being. We use those terms because the Bible uses those terms. You can always return to your objection later if you feel that the gender question remains a challenge for you personally.

* So how do we read the Bible?
In essence the way most serious Christians read the Bible is to take the text at its plainest and simplest meaning – in other words the way the writer clearly meant the words to be read and understood. We should only read the text in another way if it is quite obvious that the writer or the context demands that it be read differently. That is the approach adopted in this book.[2] Context is vital in understanding the Bible. We should not just take individual verses to "prove a point". It is rightly said that "a verse taken out of context is a pretext". When people "use" the Bible to supposedly prove a point, then if they have ripped a verse or passage out of its context, they may well be severing it from its intended meaning – and therefore they are abusing the text. This then is their 'pretext' to make the Bible say what they want it to say! Needless to say we try to avoid this error in this book.

A world in need
Hopefully the above establishes some useful foundations for us. This book, whilst it focuses on peace from a biblical

---

2 See Appendix 4. This is a useful exposition on how serious readers approach the Bible. It is borrowed, with permission, from Rev Alex Jacob's short book *Prepare the Way!* (published in 2014).

perspective, aims not to consist solely of dense text. It is said that many people are now ill-at-ease in reading dense text, as they have become more and more used to interactivity on the internet, or through the use of software packages and smart-phone apps. We will make use wherever possible of diagrams to focus on the bigger themes, but, *there is no getting away from it! God gave us a collection of 66* <u>books</u>*, plainly with the intention that we read them, study them, ponder them, discuss them, and delve into them.* If we want peace on God's terms then some effort and investment in time and energy on our part is absolutely vital. So here is the author's promise to his readers: I promise not to simply quote endless lists of verses and passages with the idea of 'proving a point'! But I will encourage readers to do exactly what the Bible implies by its very existence, to pick it up and to READ it! You may need to set aside time to do this. And you may need to switch off your mobile device(s)! The investment in time and energy should prove worthwhile. The Prince of Peace is able to – and wants to – bestow His peace universally across this planet.

The day before I began this chapter I led a family service at my local church. Our text was Luke 12:22–29. Here Jesus is telling His followers not to worry about the future:

Then Jesus said to the disciples, "And so I tell you not to worry about the food you need to stay alive or about the clothes you need for your body. Life is much more important than food, and the body much more important than clothes. Look at the crows: they don't plant seeds or gather a harvest; they don't have storage rooms or barns; God feeds them! You are worth so much more than birds! Can any of you live a bit longer by worrying about it? If you can't manage even such a small thing, why worry about the other things? Look how the wild flowers grow: they don't work or make clothes for themselves. But I tell you that not even King Solomon with all his wealth had clothes as beautiful

as one of these flowers. **It is God who clothes the wild grass – grass that is here today and gone tomorrow, burned up in the oven. Won't he be all the more sure to clothe you? What little faith you have!**

"So don't be all upset, always concerned about what you will eat and drink. (For the pagans of this world are always concerned about all these things.) Your Father knows that you need these things. Instead, be concerned with his Kingdom, and he will provide you with these things."

When we say to someone 'Don't worry', we can sometimes sound a bit glib or trite. But the words of Jesus translated into English as "so I tell you not to worry" are very different from that. They are not trite or glib, but are powerful! All of us from time to time will have difficulties and consequently things to be concerned about. Jesus understands this. After all, He lived amongst us and knows all about life's difficulties and problems. He offers us His peace, however, and this is a peace that passes all understanding. The apostle Paul wrote something similar in his letter to the Philippian church:

Don't worry about anything, but in all your prayers ask God for what you need, always asking him with a thankful heart. And God's peace, which is far beyond human understanding, will keep your hearts and minds safe in union with Christ Jesus (Philippians 4:6–7).

The "trick" here is to keep focused on God and on His commands. As Jesus said in Luke 12:29 – **Instead, be concerned with his Kingdom, and he will provide you with these things.** Jesus was speaking of the Kingdom of God, a theme that runs throughout His teaching. Once we focus on the Kingdom we begin to see things from a perspective much more aligned with God's perspective. The worries of this world begin to be replaced with the joys and certainties of the Kingdom.

At our Sunday family service we invited the grown-ups

to jot down in a few words any key worries or concerns they had, writing these on a Post-it Note before sticking them to a poster marked in large letters: "Do not worry". Having affixed them over the poster, we prayed a simple prayer referencing these Post-it Notes, asking that God would take charge of each situation in His love and mercy. Here is a selection of the things that were written:

- I worry about if there will be a war as the planes go on bombing raids.
- The world.
- The suffering people in the world – those who have no home with very little food.
- My friend's health. Mobility. Those involved in countries at war. Young people who are being abused.
- Finding a job after I have finished college.
- Family.
- My mum (half way through chemotherapy).
- Future!
- Getting old. Family that are ill.

I think these are probably a reasonable cross-section of concerns – yes, and worries – that are on the hearts and minds of so many people, even perhaps, of most people. And my church is located in a relatively safe and relatively prosperous nation. How much greater will these concerns be for people in countries at war, or suffering the scourge of terrorism, or where there is prolonged drought leading to harvest failure, or where economies are quite simply shattered – or perhaps all of these things in combination?

By comparison with these heartfelt needs and concerns, one of the UK's insurance companies in 2014 claimed to have conducted a survey amongst their customers asking them what top ten things would bring them peace of mind. Here were their published answers which, if true, show the rather trivial nature of the core concerns of many in the self-satisfied Western world.

1. **Getting rid of junk or clutter.** 'Tidy house, tidy mind' as the old adage goes.

2. **Telling someone you love them.** Don't leave it until it's too late!

3. **Organising personal effects.** Each object represents a memory and organising them not only brings back fond memories but helps loved ones making personal decisions when you're gone.

4. **Paying off the mortgage.** For most of us the largest investment we have and the one which causes the most worry. Once that's done, there is huge relief.

5. **Writing your will.** Thinking of those you'll be leaving behind and trying to make that transition worry-free is a great gift for your loved ones.

6. **Paying back someone who lent you money.** Even the smallest amount owed can lead to ill-feeling.

7. **Settling arguments with family.** After all, life is just too short....

8. **Giving back borrowed items.** Send them back, and with an apology!

9. **Having grandchildren.** Not something you can control but pure joy when it happens. All the fun without the ultimate responsibility!

10. **Making a list of music to play at your funeral**. So you can be remembered in the way you wish.

Certainly we can say that health and wealth, when they are lacking, are two concerns that can easily rob us of peace. But if all of us were healthy and wealthy would we automatically become happy, content and peaceful people? I think we all know the answer! We only have to look at the tangled lives of young sports stars or entertainers to see that health and wealth are not automatic passports to peace. We remember that an Islamist terrorist, Osama Bin Laden, was born into the family of a billionaire, yet peace was not a key feature of his life.

Cut to the Chase

Why is this book called "The Prince of Peace"? The Old Testament promises that one day a Saviour will be sent. This would be someone who would save His people from the effects and the consequences of their rebellion [sin] against God. This Saviour would swap peace for enmity, love for hate. Whilst the Old Testament is not definitive about precisely who that Saviour will be – it provides no clear name[3] – yet it certainly gives extraordinarily powerful clues about his mission and ministry. Appendix 1 to this book provides a simple table of some of these biblical "Messianic" prophecies and how disciples of Jesus believe that these prophecies were fulfilled through His life and in His ministry, via the New Testament counterpoint references. We have to acknowledge that anyone can argue against these prophecies, some complaining that they might not be prophecies at all, and others quibbling about whether Jesus was the One who actually fulfilled them. But the extraordinary linkage of prophecy and direct fulfilment in the life of one man – Jesus – looks too close for coincidence and therefore for reasonable doubt. When, even in the face of all the evidence, such doubts are still expressed, it begins to look more like avoidance of implications rather than serious objection to facts!

Prophecy means a "prediction of the future, made under divine inspiration" or a "revelation of God". The act of *making* a prophecy is the *verb*, prophesy. Of the prophecies written in the Bible about events that were to have taken place by now, we can say with confidence that each one has been fulfilled to the letter. It is difficult to make such a claim for other so-called

---

[3] Some would argue compellingly that the Old Testament does indeed provide a genealogical lineage, a name, and a curriculum vitae for Jesus – but it would take a separate book to explore these themes!

"sacred writings". The fact of fulfilled prophecy gives us confidence that God's promises for our future will be fulfilled, with equal certainty – positively, that those who place their trust in Jesus will be "saved" from the power and the effects of sin – and will go to be with Jesus forever; negatively, with the certainty that a judgement awaits all who have rejected Jesus. We will explore more of this later.

The Old Testament books in the Bible (written between 1450 BC and 430 BC) contain numerous prophecies about an "anointed one" ("Mashiach" in Hebrew) who would arrive in the future, and specifically in the land of Israel. This Messiah[4] would "deliver" or "save" the Jewish people, bringing them to paradise or heaven. These prophecies also state that the Messiah would make provision for the salvation of all the other peoples in the world "through the Jews". Specifically, for those who place their trust and faith in Jesus. For this reason, people who are *not* Jewish need to learn about this Jewish Messiah, too.

Appendix 1 to this book therefore provides a relatively small number of Messianic prophecies, pointing to the One who was to come to Israel. It is worth pausing to look at two Old Testament prophecies that speak of the future crucifixion of a suffering servant. We know that Jesus was crucified – there are references to this even in ancient secular writings. But it is the Bible that tells us, in each of the Gospel accounts of Jesus' life, that he was judicially murdered by the Romans on trumped-up charges devised by the Jerusalem religious hierarchy. How often, we might wonder, do State apparatus (in this case Rome) and religious apparatus (in this case the *second temple religious hierarchy*) combine to oppose Jesus? Is it stretching a point to suggest that much the same happens today, especially where Christians are persecuted by a religio-political combination?

Readers' attention is drawn, in this context, to Psalm 22 and to Isaiah 52:13 through 53:1–12. Both these speak powerfully

---

[4] The English word "Christ" means the same thing.

of the crucifixion of Jesus. I am going to recommend that those readers who can (and this should be most!) pause now and read each of these passages before proceeding. Then read the New Testament passages that mirror these:

Psalm 22

Isaiah 52:13–53 (all)

Matthew 27:15–66 (and John 20:31–37)

So how does Jesus' death bring me peace? How does Jesus' crucifixion and resurrection guarantee that the world can find the peace that so eludes it? We explore this in later chapters. But let us just focus now on this term "Prince of Peace". Where is this found and what does it mean?

The prophet Isaiah lived in Jerusalem in the eighth century BC. His ministry spanned a period of terrible turmoil in Israel – which was by then a divided kingdom. Isaiah lived in the southern kingdom of Judah. His prophecies concerned the threats to the people of Israel – not so much in the political fact of aggressive Assyria but also in the people's rejection of God and His designs upon their lives. Isaiah's ministry encompassed the exile of so much of the Israelite nation to Babylon, where they were crushed and without hope. Yet Isaiah told them of a future restoration, when Israel would recover their land and live again in peace. These prophecies appear to hold both short-term and long-term out-workings that are ultimately beyond the scope of this book. But in chapter 9 Isaiah speaks of a prince of peace. Let's read what he said:

The land of the tribes of Zebulun and Naphtali was once disgraced, but the future will bring honour to this region, from the Mediterranean eastward to the land on the other side of the Jordan, and even to Galilee itself, where the foreigners live. The people who walked in darkness have seen a great light. They lived in a land of shadows, but now light is shining on them. You have given them great joy, Lord; you have made them happy.

They rejoice in what you have done, as people rejoice when they harvest grain or when they divide captured wealth. For you have broken the yoke that burdened them and the rod that beat their shoulders. You have defeated the nation that oppressed and exploited your people, just as you defeated the army of Midian long ago. The boots of the invading army and all their bloodstained clothing will be destroyed by fire. A child is born to us! A son is given to us! And he will be our ruler. He will be called, "Wonderful Counsellor," "Mighty God," "Eternal Father," "Prince of Peace." His royal power will continue to grow; his kingdom will always be at peace. He will rule as King David's successor, basing his power on right and justice, from now until the end of time. The Lord Almighty is determined to do all this. (Isaiah 9:1–7).

It would be perfectly possible to write an entire book on just these seven verses, as they contain such amazing and far-reaching truths! However we will keep our review at a fairly superficial level. What is God telling us here, through Isaiah? These verses speak of the advent or the birth of a Saviour. He is a prince of peace who will go on to be the King, ruling as David's successor. This David, of course, was King David, the Hebrew king who we read about in the books *1 Samuel* and *2 Samuel* in the Old Testament. The prophet Samuel had himself prophesied that David would *always* have a dynasty, that David's kingdom will last forever. Christians recognise Jesus as David's ultimate heir – and as the resurrected Jesus still lives, so His Kingdom and Kingship can have no end. (See all of 2 Samuel 7 and specifically 2 Samuel 7:16).

To us a Son is given. Jesus is given to the entire world, although Isaiah 9:1–7 is speaking primarily to Isaiah's Hebrew readership – the first temple nation of Judah, which is about to face an unprecedented calamity – military defeat and exile. But to them (and to us) a Son will be given and He will be our ultimate ruler. He will be known as **Wonderful**

Counsellor – certainly a reflection of Jesus' wisdom and truthfulness, but also possibly an allusion to the fact that He and the Holy Spirit are inextricably linked. It is the Holy Spirit who Jesus promises to send to His followers – and in John 14:26 Jesus specifically refers to the Spirit as the counsellor. If readers want to delve into this aspect of Jesus' ministry then they should pause now and read John 14:15–31. ⬜

This Son who will be given will be known as "Mighty God", "Eternal Father" and "Prince of Peace". The promise is affirmed – that His royal power will continue to increase and His Kingdom will always be at peace. In this idea of *increase*, Christians see two factors at work – first, that all through history people have loved Jesus and chosen to respond to Him by following Him as His faithful disciples. In this sense the number of disciples down through history continue to expand – now into the billions. And second, that in spite of worldly opposition, the influence of the church also expands, acting as "salt" and "light" in society – whether or not that society welcomes this flavouring and illumination.

The notion that the Son's kingdom will always be at peace may be considered problematic: the reality of opposition and persecution is painfully true to Christians. In this context 'peace' surely does not mean an absence of hardship or opposition, rather it means a positive reality that, in spite of the worst that the world can do (and the worst that the devil can do), individual Christians[5] have a sense of peace that this world simply cannot rival. In this way Jesus' Kingdom is always at peace. Our hearts are at peace as we know Him in Whom we place our trust and He Who has already paid the great debt that we owe. And one day, of course, when Jesus

---

[5] When we refer to "Christians" in this book, generally we do so in the clear sense that these are genuine believers in, and disciples of, Jesus. People who say with their lips – and mean in their hearts – that JESUS IS LORD. We do not mean this term in the political or cultural sense. People who think of themselves a "Christians" by default, will not enjoy the sense of ultimate peace which this book explores.

returns, His disciples will be granted permanent existential peace.

It is from the prophet Isaiah, then, that we receive this wonderful title – and this wonderful truth – that Jesus is the Prince of Peace. Isaiah tells us that He (Jesus) will rule as King David's successor, basing his power on right and justice. It is on the justice and righteousness of God, as much as the love of God, that we found our future hope of peace. God WILL do the right thing. And as Isaiah says: "**The Lord Almighty is determined to do all this**". Halleluiah!

Chapter Two

WHAT IS PEACE?

God's peace or the world's peace?

In the UK in the 1980s there emerged a political movement which focused on the military airbase at RAF Greenham Common (actually an American base under lease arrangements from the RAF). A group of women established in 1981 a makeshift "peace camp" outside the perimeter of the base to protest and be a focal point for agitation against the deployment of 96 cruise missiles which had been developed and deployed as a counter-balance to the earlier Russian deployment of SS20 intermediate range nuclear missiles (threatening western Europe) within the Russian sphere of influence, known as the Warsaw Pact territories. The "Women of Greenham Common" saw themselves as peace-makers and they initiated a form of segregated communal living that lasted for 19 years. Their activities centred on various civil disobedience measures, resulting inevitably in arrests and some convictions. They excluded males from their protest movement, much to the amusement of some sections of the press and media, yet they had a serious purpose. Whether their activities were right and appropriate is for historians to judge. In fact their movement seems to have made no difference to the eventual outcome, which was that the SS20 nuclear threat was faced-down and Russia eventually became semi-bankrupt in its determination to prosecute an arms race against the Western powers. The Berlin wall fell in 1989 and European communism effectively died.

Were the peace protesters a help or a hindrance to politicians trying to broker peace? And what does peace mean to such "roots-based" agitators? Peace, for these people, seems to mean an end to warfare, which some see as a peculiar feature of patriarchal societies – that is, societies "dominated" by men. It will be seen that each of these phrases, 'end to warfare', 'patriarchal societies' and 'dominated by men' are heavily-loaded and mean different things to different people. What is the Bible's broad approach to the question of peace? Is there a consistent view about peace within the Bible?

We need to begin this "study" (for that is what it will be) by stating quite simply that "peace" is what the Bible tells us that God, as Creator, wants to give to us. It is perhaps interesting that the very first words recorded as having been expressed by God to a man (and by implication to mankind) are "be fruitful" (Genesis 1:28) which, by implication, surely includes the idea of peaceful well-being. Additionally, the first words recorded to Adam (Genesis 2:16) are words that indicate that God is handing over a good measure of freedom to humans. In the NIV we read "you are free...." This is useful, if perhaps somewhat a paraphrase of the text which is better translated as "you may freely". But either translation gives us the same sense, that there is a liberality at the heart of God's purposes. What is going on here in Genesis chapter 2?

Genesis is the first book in the Bible – the first in the Old Testament. It is the first book of "the promise", if you prefer. Having pointed out in the previous chapter that some readers may have real issues and problems if they do not actually believe in God, we immediately hit a fresh problem in this second chapter: some readers may have difficulty with the Bible's account of Creation. Let me respond with a thought about the book of Genesis. Some Christians consider the book to be literally true and linearly true. In other words the events described happened in the way described and in the order described. They take Genesis at its plainest possible reading. Others consider that the book reveals "truths" that are plain to see but not necessarily meant to be understood in a linear way – in other words the things described actually happened but not necessarily in a physical sense, nor necessarily in a linear time-ordered sense.

Whichever way a reader chooses to look at Genesis, it does not make a big difference to the arguments set out in this book. There is a third way of reading and understanding Genesis, which is that both positions are true at the same time! Now this completely surprising thought takes some prayerful effort to really enter into. We only consider it here as there is a case for saying that, sometimes, positions that appear to be mutually exclusive are *not in fact* mutually exclusive. Some have described such an approach a *Hebraic mindset* which is opposed to and in contrast to the Western "Greek" mindset, a mindset which totally dominates our modern world. Incidentally, your author is *not* suggesting that a Hebraic mindset *would* find that both the literal and metaphorical interpretations of Genesis are equally true. This is only suggested as it helps us to bypass an immediate and substantial 'problem' for some people – that of 'Creation' versus some other way of explaining our existence here on planet earth.

The author's view on Creation, for what it is worth, is not crucial to how this book develops its key themes. But he wants his readers to mark this. What Genesis tells us, emphatically, is that:

- [ ] God created the world (*how* is not relevant to this book).
- [ ] God created it with a good purpose.
- [ ] God created it perfectly – such troubles as we recognise in the world result from mankind's resistance to God.
- [ ] God created men and women for each other.[1]

God's creation purposes are set out in Genesis chapters 1 and 2. Peace seems to be at the heart of what God wants for

---

[1] This is a subject explored fully in the author's earlier book *One Flesh – what Jesus teaches about love, relationships, marriage and a lot more.* Google Glory to Glory Publications to download a free edition.

His Creation and peace is emphatically what God ordains into eternity for His true followers. Those who are His loyal servants and who accept the gift of His Son will be granted both an eternal life with that same Son, and eternal peace. These are huge statements to make. It is hoped that the remainder of this book will give clear grounds for confidence in the truthfulness of these basic assertions about God's heart and God's purposes. The world's idea of peace is simply at odds with what Jesus said and what the Bible more generally reveals.

What then can we say about the Bible's understanding of peace? Peace is total well-being, security and prosperity associated with God's presence amongst His people. It is inextricably linked in the Old Testament with the covenants. Please refer to Appendix 2 to explore the various covenants and how they interact with each other. It is generally understood that the promise of peace is most closely identified with the Messianic covenant, which promises life from death to all mankind, subject only to obedience measured in terms of relationship to the suffering servant. This gift of life will be *brought* by a Saviour, who will be from the house and lineage of King David. This gift of life will be *bought* by a Saviour, (not a spelling mistake!) at the cost of His own life. Measured through the covenants, the presence of peace as God's gift is conditional upon Israel's obedience. Prophetically, in terms of prophecy as yet to be fulfilled, peace is part of the end-time hope of God's salvation. In the New Testament this peace is understood to come solely through Jesus, the Messiah, and is experienced by faith in Him.

Peace in the Old Testament – The Promise
Jewish people correctly call the Old Testament the *Tanakh*. **Shalom** is the term most often translated as "peace" in the Tanakh. In this Old Testament of our modern Bibles, or *promise* as some call it, *shalom* holds a wide range of meanings – wholeness, health, security, well-being, and

salvation. And shalom can apply to a wide range of contexts – the state of the individual (Psalm 37:37; Proverbs 3:2; Isaiah 32:17), the relationship of man to man (Genesis 34:21; Joshua 9:15), and the relationship of God to man (Psalm 85:8; Jeremiah 16:5).

The following definition from the 2011 (*One New Man* translation of the Bible; published by True Potential Publishing Inc in the USA) explores *shalom* and its opposite: 'Shalom cannot be translated into English with a single word. Shalom comes from Shalem meaning to be complete. When there is shalom there is tranquillity, justice, sufficient food, clothing, housing. There is divine health, with no sickness. Shalom means an absence of: disorder, injustice, bribery, corruption, conflict, lack, hatred, abuse, violence, pain, suffering, immorality, and all other negative forces. A rabbi wrote that shalom means "no good thing is withheld". Therefore when we pray for the shalom of Jerusalem we are praying that there will not be any injustice, disorder, strife, violence, poverty, sickness, abuse, accidents, homelessness, pain, hunger, and more. When shalom reigns there will be no immorality, no injustice. The principles advocated in the Torah will be followed by all. Then the command to love your neighbour will be made complete.'[2]

It will be seen that this is a much more expansive understanding of peace than merely the absence of conflict. It has about it the idea of humans and God in harmony – with humans living as God intended. Remember in the Genesis account of Creation, at the end of each fresh aspect of creation God announces "it is good". God created with a good purpose and He desires the best for all humans. To quote again from the One New Man Bible ("ONMB"), there is a counterpoint to shalom: "**Ra** (Resh-Ayin) is the opposite of shalom. While Ra is commonly translated evil or wicked, bad is given as the first meaning. The dictionary does not express the real

---

[2] Glossary – One New Man Bible (True Potential Publishing, Inc, copyright 2011, with permission).

meaning and English has no simple meaning for the Hebrew word Ra. Ra is the opposite of shalom, so it means that *nothing makes sense* or fits. Chaos and anarchy are often used in this translation because they may best express the meaning of Ra. Anarchy or chaos reigned when the children of Israel strayed after false gods, when the seasons of the Lord and tithes were ignored. When there is chaos in society bullies take over, so might makes right. Corruption and bribery are common.[3] Freedom is restricted. Immorality is the norm. There is no order in society, no justice. Sometimes in our lives we find that even though we cannot put a finger on it, there is just a feeling of things not right. That is the mild side of Ra. The far end of Ra is when *everything is wrong*, as with an absolutely hopeless situation. In that case only a personal relationship with the Living God can give you peace in your spirit. Through Him you can make it."

William Morford, translator of the ONMB, makes a telling point in the above. The peace that God offers is based on relationship. It is sometimes said that *true biblical Christianity is not so much a religion as a relationship*. A relationship of a righteous God who reaches down into our situation with mercy, deep concern and love. We in turn respond to that mercy and love with our own love and loyalty, living by the standards that He set out for us. It is in this way that we encounter and discover that true peace, in contra-distinction to the false worldly peace so often peddled to us. How can people in the UK forget the hapless Prime Minister Neville Chamberlain who, after the Munich Crisis in September 1938, returned to Heston airport[4] and waved a piece of paper above his head announcing "peace for our time", barely twelve

---

[3] EDITOR'S NOTE: It is interesting that world development experts are beginning to identify systemic corruption in developing countries as the main brake upon social and legal development across the developing world.

[4] Today, Heathrow Airport

months before the beginning of the Second World War?[5] It is for this misjudgement that Chamberlain is principally remembered today.

In the Old Testament, with its insistent promise of a future Saviour, the presence of shalom is not considered ultimately to be the "fruit" of human endeavour, but rather it is seen as being a gift or blessing from God (see Leviticus 26:6; 1 Kings 2:33; Job 25:2; Psalm 29:11, etc). Peace therefore is also tied in closely with the reality of covenant. There are five covenants distinctly recorded in the Old Testament (see again Appendix 2). These covenants are entered into by God with mankind. God always initiates the covenant and the special feature of all these covenants is that God guarantees to keep them, whether or not humans fulfil their obligations. But some covenants have conditions! The covenants, at the most basic, are God's principal way of interacting with humankind. So, God promises that the world will continue until such time as God determines to end it. God has chosen a people (the Hebrews) to be His special ambassadors in this world.[6] God promises specifically that the Hebrews are to be a kingdom of priests and a blessing to the whole world (the "Moses Covenant"). God knew that the Hebrews would

---

[5] **"Peace for Our Time"** – the phrase echoed Benjamin Disraeli, who upon returning from the Congress of Berlin in 1878 stated "I have returned from Germany with peace for our time." Often misquoted as "peace *in* our time", which had appeared long before in the Book of Common Prayer as "Give peace in our time, O Lord", probably based on the 7th-century hymn 'Da pacem Domine! in diebus nostris, Alleluja'. It is unknown how deliberate was Chamberlain's use of such a similar term, but anyone of his background would have been familiar with the original.

[6] Christians argue, convincingly, that it being in-grafted to the Hebrew root, they now share and largely assume that role as God's ambassadors, and will continue to be the primary ambassadors of God's Kingdom of Grace until such time as the "full number" of Jews have come into covenant relationship with their Messiah. Romans chapters 9 through 11 speak powerfully into this.

fail in this holy task, just as any other nation would have failed. So God had already set in place a "new covenant" (otherwise popularly known as the "Messianic Covenant") which focuses on receiving God's blessing through one Man – the second Adam, Jesus. Appendix 2 should help readers to get a sense of the broad sweep of the reality of covenant. Readers are encouraged to obtain two other really helpful books that explore this subject in greater detail. A useful introductory text is David Pawson's *By God, I Will – The Biblical Covenants*. Kelvin Crombie's masterly and expansive text is *In Covenant With Jesus*. See the *Further Reading* list at the back of this book for full details. We can say, in summary, that the covenants are vital to understanding God's ultimate Salvation purposes.

Peace, then, in the Old Testament is closely tied-in with the reality of Covenant. Shalom is the desired outcome of true communion and harmony between the two covenant partners (God and Israel – see Numbers 6:26; Isaiah 54:10–17). The presence of shalom is indicative of blessings within the covenant relationship (Malachi 2:5; cf. Numbers 25:12) whilst the absence of shalom is seen as being a result of Israel's unrighteousness and disobedience (Jeremiah 16:5; Jeremiah 16:10–13; Psalm 85:9–13; Isaiah 32:17). Sadly, much of the Old Testament/Tanakh/Promise revolves around what became a frequently broken relationship, with Israel constantly tempted to chase after other "gods" in preference to the true God who is the God of Abraham, Isaac and Jacob – those founding fathers of the Hebrew nation (Exodus 3:6; Acts 3:13).

Shalom is a key term in the writings of the prophets. It would be the "false" prophets who, ignoring the conditions for national well being within the covenant relationship, presumed upon God's unconditional loyalty to Israel (see Psalm 89) and that this loyalty would guarantee peace (Jeremiah 6:14; 8:15; Ezekiel 13:10, 16; Micah 3:5). A quick glance at Appendix 2 shows that the key *Moses covenant* is indeed a conditional one – it is conditional upon Israel's obedience to the terms of that covenant. Against the popular but false notion of national security, the pre-exile prophets warned about the coming judgement, precisely because of Israel's persistent disobedience and associated unrighteousness (Isaiah 48:18; Jeremiah 14:13–16; 16:5, 10–13, 28; Micah 3:4, 9–12).

There would be, however, a future time of unprecedented shalom for Israel, characterised by prosperity and well-being (Isaiah 45:7; Ezekiel 34:25–6) and absence of warfare (Isaiah 2:2–4; 32:15–20; Ezekiel 34:28–31; Hosea 2:18–23). This wonderful shalom would incorporate:
* right relationships (Isaiah 11:1–5; Micah 4:1–4; Zechariah 8:9–13)
* restoration of harmony in nature (Isaiah 11:6-9; Ezra 47:1–12)
* salvation (Isaiah 52:7; 60:17; Ezekiel 34:30–1; 37:26–8)

Very often this end-time scenario painted by the prophets would include the Messianic figure, as in Isaiah 9:6 where He is referred to as "The Prince of Peace". And His reign will be one of peace, not only for Israel, but will extend across the globe (Zechariah 9:9–10). The Tanakh ends with this hope of peace still unrealised in its fullest sense.

Peace in the New Testament – the Promise Fulfilled

The Greek term for peace used in the New Testament is usually *irene*, a word enlarged from its classical Greek connotation with "rest" to encompass the various ideas associated with shalom, explored above. Like the word *shalom*, *irene* could be used as:
* a greeting or farewell (as in "peace be with you" – Luke 10:5; Galatians 6:16; James 2:16; John 20:19),
* a reference to domestic tranquillity (1 Corinthians 7:15–16)
* a reference to the ceasing of war (Luke 14:32; Acts 12:20)
* a reference to the absence of interpersonal squabbles (Romans 14:19; Ephesians 4:3)

In the New Testament (or *Promise Fulfilled* as some like to think of it) the main question is: how does Jesus fulfil the Old Testament hope for that eschatological (end-time) peace of God? In the prophecy of Zechariah, recorded for us in Luke 1:67–79, the coming of Jesus will "**guide our steps into the path of peace**" (v. 79, GNB). The Angels at Messiah Jesus' birth proclaim Jesus to be the bringer of peace to Mankind. "**Glory to God in the highest heaven, and on earth peace to those with whom he is pleased**" (Luke 2:14). In this the angels confirm that Jesus will usher in God's reign of true shalom, the time of "salvation" that had been longed for since the time of the prophets. Jesus' own expression of his legacy as recorded in the Gospel[7] of John makes the promise: "**Peace is what I leave with you; it is my own peace that I give to you. I do not give it as the world does....**" We will return to this later, but for now we mark simply that Jesus promises *His* brand of peace, and that is at odds with the world's ideas of peace.

We can explore the nature of this gift of Jesus' peace first by stating what it is not. It is not 'peace' as the world understands it. Indeed Jesus said in another context (which we will explore later) something quite astounding: "**Do not think I have come to bring peace to the world. No, I did not come to bring peace, but a sword. I came to set sons against their fathers, daughters against their mothers, daughters-in-law against their mothers-in-law; a man's worst enemies will become his friends**". (Matthew 10:34–36 GNB; see also Luke 12:51–53; 14:26–27). So Jesus' peace is not an end to tension, or domestic tranquillity, or an end to warfare, nor anything like the world's estimation of peace. Jesus' presence in our lives may, in contrast, upset existing relationships, bringing a dividing "sword" into family relationships. Jesus' legacy of peace is, in truth, the reality of the new covenant in His blood, which reconciles Man to God (Romans 5:1; Colossians 1:20) and forms the basis of

---

[7] "Gospel" is the normal term applied to the four life histories of Jesus i.e. the books of Matthew, Mark, Luke and John in the New Testament.

true reconciliation between people under their Messiah (see Ephesians 2:14–22).

The New Testament church certainly understood "peace" in precisely this way – as the final end-time salvation of God given already through Jesus the Messiah (cf Philippians 4:7, 9). Peter preached "peace with God", through Jesus the Messiah (Acts 10:36–7) and Paul similarly preached Jesus as "our peace" bringing near to God those who had formerly been far away (Ephesians 2:13–14; 6:15). The distinctive "Christian" understanding of peace transformed the friendly farewell "go in peace", which was taken up by believers as their way of saying *go, and be blessed in the power and certainty of Jesus*. The apostle Paul frequently used his "grace and peace" greeting at the commencement of his letters to the early churches (e.g. 1 Corinthians 1:3, Galatians 1:3; Ephesians 1:2; etc, also 1 Peter 1:2, 2 John 3; Jude 2, Revelation 1:4). This is why at the end of modern Christian church services, very often the congregation will be invited to "go in peace", with the prayer that this peace will "protect your hearts and minds" in the "knowledge and love of Jesus".

We can affirm, then, that it is no mere hopeful wish for peace which Paul offers his readers. It is, instead, a solid reminder of the messianic gifts available to all humans in the present day through discipleship of Jesus. Jesus gives His peace and we will explore in a later chapter how that works out in practice. Jesus is described as "peace" itself (Ephesians 2:14) whilst God, because of His act of reconciliation through Jesus the Messiah, is known as the "God of peace" (Philippians 4:9; Colossians 3:15). The gift of peace through reconciliation with God is in turn obtained by trusting in Jesus. But this does, however, place a real ethical demand on Christians. It calls, firstly, for the constant exercise of "peace" – for example in reconciliation between individuals within the church, and wherever possible outside the church as well. Lastly peace is a recognised "fruit" of the Holy Spirit – and as a fruit it should grow "naturally" as a by-product of the

Christian life (Galatians 5:22). Peace is to be the objective of the Christian in their relationships with others (Romans 12:18; 14:19; Hebrews 12:14, etc) and those who actively work for true peace – and we must emphasise it is *true* peace that we are discussing – will be marked out as "children of God" (Matthew 5:9).

Being Sure
How can we be sure that God desires to give us peace? In this troubled world in which we live, and which Christians say that God created, why is it that peace is so conspicuous by its absence? Your author believes that we can indeed be *sure* that God desires to give us peace – as we only have to look at Jesus to see the perfect mirror of God's full nature. If we want to know what God looks like, then we look at Jesus (see Colossians 1:15). Christians would say three things about the revealed nature of God:

1. He is good
2. He is holy
3. He is righteous

It is probably true that most people will have some sense of what these things mean so I will not try to spell them out here. In an earlier book, looking at whether peace can be found in the contemporary supposed and popular "promise" of all the religions combined in hoped-for harmony, I included specific chapters titled "Is God Good?" and "Is God Holy?" Readers who want to explore this in greater detail are encouraged to look out *The Empty Promise of Godism*.[8] I would merely point out here that there are at least *some* churchgoers who do not believe that God is totally good, and accordingly do not

---

[8] *The Empty Promise of Godism – Reflections on the Multifaith Agenda* by Peter Sammons. Refer to the further reading list at the back of this book. At time of writing the book is freely available chapter by chapter as PDF files via www.glorytoglory.co.uk

believe that He is holy. I will not argue against this here. For a churchgoer to adopt such a mindset is odd – in the light of all that the Gospels teach us about God – and raises the possibility that those who adhere to this view are mirroring their own sins back upon God – effectively blaming Him for them! This is a truly odd position to adopt – especially if one calls oneself a "Christian". God is indeed good, and He desires good for us. God is holy, He is altogether *other* – set apart from us and morally upright. (We are not!) And God is *righteous*. What does this mean? It means simply that what He does is right – completely right and completely trustworthy. When God is described in the Bible, it is generally as a *righteous* God, not so often the 'loving' God that is the preferred motif of so many of our modern churches. Jesus prayed to His righteous Father (John 17:25) but never to a loving Father, so far as we know – for there is no such reference in the Bible. This is not to suggest that God is unloving or parsimonious in His love – far from it. But the English word 'love' is a slippery one and open to considerable misinterpretation. Please refer to Appendix 3 on the wonderful subject of God's love. A *righteous* God will always and unswervingly do the right thing – the completely right thing – and so He is completely trustworthy.

But we cannot ignore the inconvenient truth that it is often the good, and very often the innocent, who seem to suffer in this world. There are murders daily in most countries on the plant. There are wars and rumours of wars. Sickness, hunger, want and ignorance abound in this world. And one in ten of Christians on the face of this planet live in conditions of foul persecution – either religious or political, or both combined. Is it then glib to talk about a merciful God who sends peace, when those who are innocently loyal to Him suffer unspeakably? That is a fair question that we must confront as the Prince of Peace invites us to follow Him.

As we begin to address this question, which defies a simple answer, we need to note the whole sweep of the biblical revelation of God and His holy purposes. In contra-distinction to most of the world's religions, true biblical Christianity has a simple meta-narrative – a story that has a beginning, a middle and an end. No matter how complex the Bible may seem at first glance, it is actually saying something relatively straightforward to us. It is telling us that, having created this world and its inhabitants, God has a good plan to bring out the very best for us. He graciously allows us a measure of free-will – specifically the free will to accept Him or to reject Him. He refuses to force Himself upon us. He desires a relationship with us, not the relationship of a technician to a robot that he has constructed, but the relationship of a God who reaches down into our daily situations, with the objective of giving us a permanent home with Him for eternity. The relationship He seeks is one of mutual love, although the nature of the loves expressed on both sides is fundamentally different. God's love for us is a righteous love best expressed by the Greek word *agape*. Our love expressed in return is best expressed in the Greek word *phileo* [although agape is a part of this]. God's objective of giving us a permanent home with Him, a permanent relationship, is met through progressive revelation, first through a chosen people, and latterly through His own Son. This meta-narrative can be expressed in Fig. 1 (below).

It has rightly been said that all history is, in reality, *His*-story. It is hoped that the diagram of Salvation History (below) sets out in relatively straightforward terms what the Bible reveals. This is the Bible's meta-narrative – its "big story". Some historians and theologians might quibble with aspects of the way this has been set out, but it is hoped that most will see this as a reasonable summary that sets out the basic 'topography' (or the high points) of God's overall revelatory purpose. It is a story that moves inexorably from rebellion to peace, a story worked out in a people and in a Man. God's purpose then, is thoroughly good. And the outcome of God's purpose is peace – and this is a peace that passes all understanding (see Philippians 4:7). But the world at large does not share that design for peace, or even that desire for peace. The world at large wants "peace" on its own terms – and this it cannot have.

SALVATION HISTORY – THE CALL TO PEACE

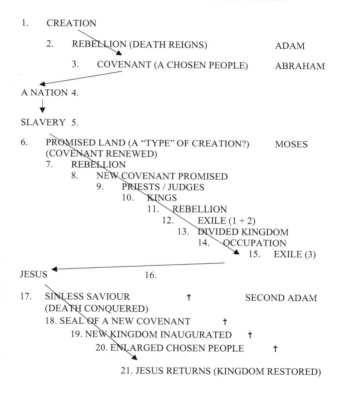

Fig. 1

SALVATION HISTORY – THE CALL TO PEACE
Biblical references illustrating the sweep of Salvation History:

1. Gen 1–2; Ps 33:6–9; Isa 50:2–3; Job 38:1–18
2. Gen 3
3. Gen 12:1–9; Gen 15:1–21; Gen 17:1–14
4. Gen 12:2–3; Ps 33:12
5. Ex 1–12 inclusive
6. Josh 1:1–9; 12 inclusive; 13:1–7; Ps 105:6; Isa 41:9
7. Throughout Old Testament (Tanakh)
8. Jeremiah 31:31–33; See also Appendix 2 – A Covenant Keeping God
9. Judges / 1 Samuel 1–7 inclusive
10. 1 Samuel 8 inclusive; 1 Sam 16:1–13; 1 and 2 Kings inclusive;
2 Chronicles 36:5–8
11. 1 and 2 Kings inclusive
12. 2 Chronicles 36:13–23; [Babylonian 1] Jeremiah 52:1–34 [Babylonian 2]
13. 2 Chronicles 10:1–19
14. Roman occupation is not explained in Scripture, although there are allusions to it.
15. Exile under Rome is not recorded in Scripture. Exile alluded to by Jesus in Matthew 24. Revelation 16:1–7 may prefigure the Roman exile.
16. Matthew, Mark, Luke, John (Gospels) inclusive
17. 1 John 2:2; 1 John 1:5–7; Coloss 2:9–15; Philippians 2:6–11; Coloss 1:15–23
18. Matt 26:26–30; Luke 22:17–20; 1 Cor 11:23–25; Rev 5:6–14
19. Matt 6:33; Matt 12:28; Luke 11:20; Matt 8:11; Acts 1:6–8. There are several levels of meaning to "Kingdom".
20. Romans 9–11 inclusive; Romans 11:11–24 especially; Galatians 3:26–29; Ephesians 4:4–5; Rev 7:8–10; Rev 14:6–7
21. Rev 19:1–9; Rev 21:1–7; Rev 22:7–17; Acts 1:11

A note on the biblical references:
These references are the author's personal selection. Many others might have been selected to illustrate the same points, but hopefully these contain sufficient directness and precision to emphasize the broad roadmap of Salvation History.

A note on the periods of exile:
Deportation of defeated enemy leaders was a common feature of both Assyrian and Babylonian empires. In the Bible the term "the exile" or "captivity" refers to the deportation of Judah's leaders from Jerusalem in the 6th century BC. Earlier, the leaders of the Northern Kingdom (Israel) had been deported by the Assyrians, following the fall of Samaria in 722 BC.

Chapter Three

THE ROAD MAP TO PEACE

The Gospel and the Church

In this chapter we will simply look at what it means to become a disciple of Jesus – a follower of Jesus. Readers might ask – why? Why do so now? Should this subject not be an appendix to this wider study of peace? We will turn our attention to the reality and the process of what the Bible calls Salvation because, without Salvation, ultimate and true peace cannot be enjoyed – or even experienced. Once we have focused on Salvation, then this becomes the backdrop against which we will explore other aspects of peace and how it is attained and maintained. Without looking at Salvation now, it will remain "the elephant in the room" as we explore peace, and will become an "itch" that needs to be scratched, sooner or later! So let us explore this now. Let us scratch that "itch", albeit this theme of Salvation will resurface several times in this book.

It is surprisingly difficult to summarise what the good news (or gospel) actually is, in the sense of speaking definitively and with absolute precision. Sadly there is evidence that some churches offer to the world a watered-down, user-friendly "gospel", often focused around what is called a *social gospel* – the false, but to some a superficially attractive idea, that God wants us to create by our own efforts a happy world. Now, dear reader, I would ask you, if you are a church attending Christian, if you can summarise to yourself, perhaps using a key verse from the Bible, what is the gospel? You might want to pause just now for a moment to consider this. If there is one Bible verse above all others that is likely to spring to mind, you might name it now – book, chapter and verse! If there is such a single 'gospel in a nutshell' then many would consider it to be John 3:16. Is this, however, the gospel? David Pawson argues powerfully that it is not, in his two short books; *Is John 3:16 the Gospel?* and *The God and the Gospel of Righteousness* (both widely available at the time of writing this book, and both used as inspiration in the following section).

The gospel is often presented along these lines: *God loves you, has a wonderful plan for your life, and will accept you if you, in turn, accept Jesus.* Some churches do not even go that far! Some now teach that God accepts you whoever you are, whatever you have done and in whatever state you finally leave this world! This is called 'universalism' and runs along the lines 'God is so loving that even Hitler[1] will be saved!' But is this what Jesus taught?

There seem to be three gospel schemes in wide circulation and we will present them in summary form, so I apologise in advance to my readers for what may be considered great imprecision! However, readers will hopefully quickly see the point of this and how this chimes with our wider theme of the pursuit of true peace. What, then, is *the good news*? Is it simply that God loves you? If your answer is yes then the "gospel" goes something like this (scheme A)

- ☐ I was born a scoundrel
- ☐ I lived the life of a scoundrel
- ☐ I died a scoundrel
- ☐ But that's all right because God loves me!

This is perhaps the idea of universalism. It evolves into a philosophy that makes "god" a sort of easy going grandfather-in-the-sky deity who is not fussed about your religion (as "he" owns them all!) and will "save" everyone through Jesus. Does your church teach this "gospel"?

---

[1] For those who do not know, Adolf Hitler was the German dictator who began the Second World War in 1939 – a war that cost some 30 million people their lives in Europe alone, and millions elsewhere.

The above might be modified slightly in this way (scheme B)

- [ ] I was born a scoundrel
- [ ] I lived the life of a scoundrel
- [ ] I became a Christian so then I led a somewhat better life
- [ ] I died not as bad as I began!
- [ ] But that's all right because God loves me!

Is *this* all there is to it? Attending at least some churches, we could be excused for thinking it is. The only verse every Christian is pretty much guaranteed to know off by heart, as we have seen, is John 3:16, but many consider that this verse has been taken out of context and is mis-applied. More traditional churches might render the gospel in this way (scheme C):

- [ ] I was born a scoundrel
- [ ] I lived the life of a scoundrel
- [ ] I met Jesus and received Him into my life [Justification] and Jesus progressively made me more like Him
- [ ] My subsequent life was one of joy and service [Sanctification]
- [ ] God receives me because Jesus died in my place

Scheme C is closer to the biblical ideal, to be sure. But it is still highly transactional in its approach and therefore seems to sell the good news short – and that in turn means to sell Jesus short. In Scheme C we included two technical theological words [in brackets] which helpfully describe the process with a little more precision. Indeed, Scheme C acknowledges salvation as being a journey, rather than as an event. It is writer Mike Endicott who helpfully speaks of *the gate of justification* leading on to *the road to sanctification* (see Further Reading – *Kingdom Seekers*). Even in Scheme C, as we have colloquially summarised it, we have not really identified just what it is that God graciously offers which we as individuals have the option to accept or reject. If there is a key and unbridgeable distinction between biblical Christianity and *the religions* (e.g. Islam, Buddism, Hinduism, Judaism, etc) it must be this: Christianity is highly personal in the sense that God offers an opportunity which Jesus gives to be 'born again', which at a personal level you either accept or reject (and rejection does not have to be a positive thing – it can also be quite simply in ignoring the wonderful offer that has been made – ignoring the cross of Jesus). The religions by contrast always see an individual as being born into their religion and from which they may not escape (except in some cases, at the risk of rejection and death). The individual is subsumed into their community and is not known by their god as distinct – hence the Islamic concept of the *umma* for example – that community of followers of Allah – where the community assumes responsibility for the individual. And hence no individual or personal relationship of child to parent can be experienced. No Muslim or Hindu could ever call God "Abba" as can a believer in Jesus (Galatians 4:6–7).

It is fair to say that God was never known as "Father" until Jesus came to earth and revealed Him in this way. In His prayer to His Father, Jesus said, "**I have made you** [your name] **known to them, and will continue to make you known in order that the love that you have for me may be in them and that I myself may be in them**" (John 17:26) To what name was Jesus referring? It was the name "Father". If there is anything central to Jesus' heart, it is to introduce us to God as "Father". Elsewhere Jesus said, "**do not worry, saying, 'What shall we eat?' or 'What shall we drink?' or 'What shall we wear?' For your heavenly Father knows that you need them**" (Matthew 6:31–32). In addition, He said, "**If you then, being evil, know how to give good gifts to your children, how much more will your Father who is in heaven give good things to those who ask Him!**" (Matthew 7:11). We can say emphatically, then, that to know God through Jesus is to know God as Father.

Perhaps a more accurate way of thinking about the gospel

message than is highlighted in our schemes A, B and C above, is to express this divine exchange (Jesus taking our punishment on Himself) more in terms of what is *given* to the believer as well as what is *taken away* from him or her. The flaw in the above schemes, even Scheme C, is that they do not go far enough! Even with justification sorted out, and with the journey of sanctification safely embarked upon, if you were to die tonight – and indeed if I was to die tonight – why on earth should God have you or me anywhere near Him? We know from Jesus that only people who are completely right before God will be with Him for eternity (Revelation 21:27). I know I am not completely right before God – and if I may risk offending my readers, I know that you are not completely right either! We will never be completely right in this life, so we can never enter *that place* where absolutely everything is right, because if we did, then we would simply pollute it. We would spoil it. It would no longer be holy and accordingly neither God nor His Holy Spirit would abide there. So what is the remedy? How is this eternal conundrum finally and permanently resolved? Plainly it is not by keeping God's holy laws,[2] because we cannot do it, we are simply incapable of doing it. God's chosen people (the Hebrews) were given God's Torah and the responsibility to live it as a sort of spiritual prototype on behalf of all mankind, blazing a trail of obedience that the rest of humanity might follow! The Hebrews failed, just as any other nation would have failed. That is why God always had in mind the new and better covenant, inaugurated by the blood of Jesus the Messiah Himself.

What is this better alternative, this good news? What does Christianity offer that 'the religions' cannot? What does the gospel offer? We learn from the apostle Paul: **I am not ashamed of the gospel, because it is the power of God for the salvation of everyone who believes: first for the Jew, then for the Gentile. For in the gospel a *righteousness* from**

---

[2] More correctly known as Torah – or "teaching".

God is revealed, a *righteousness* that is by faith from first to last, just as it is written: "The *righteous* will live by faith." (Romans 1:16–17; emphasis by author). Three times here is the offer of righteousness. We can never make it on our own. We can never make ourselves righteous enough. But God offers us His righteousness! God is showing us that we will never have enough of our own, so instead the **gospel of God** (Romans 1:1) offers to us the righteousness of God Himself, given by grace (meaning: an undeserved gift) obtained through faith in Jesus' crucifixion and resurrection.

We can say that God's righteousness is **imputed** to us when we are born again, when we receive Jesus as our Lord and Saviour, and God's righteousness is **imparted** to us progressively as we go through life. So, we are saved as we are justified by faith, and are justified by the Judge – God. We are justified – a legal term – and Jesus' righteousness is *imputed* to us. God's righteousness is *imparted* progressively to us as we walk in His strength and holiness. Remember what Jesus said: **narrow is the road that leads to life, and only a few find it** (Matthew 7: 14). By faithfully treading that pathway, we become progressively more like our Saviour. That is *imparted* righteousness – from the Holy Spirit, imparted to the disciples of Jesus.

Righteousness is *imputed* through Jesus and *imparted* through the Holy Spirit. It is rightly said, that all three Persons in the Trinity are involved in this process of Salvation. Imputed righteousness represents and explains God's forgiveness of our past sinful life. If God were to forgive our sin without any conditions it would be unrighteous of Him to do so. And yet He pronounces us saints because of Jesus and what Jesus has achieved. There is no such thing as unconditional forgiveness. It would be wrong for a good and righteous God to forgive sins unless two conditions were met. Firstly, *that our sins should have been paid for already* – which is what Jesus has done for us. The heart of the gospel is that Jesus has already paid. This is why there can be no forgiveness without the cross. We can say emphatically that every act of forgiveness is written in the blood of Jesus. That is what my forgiveness and your forgiveness actually cost. But there is a second condition, on our side: *we are to repent*. It would be immoral of God to forgive our sins in the absence of true repentance. Repentance is something we do – it is a change of lifestyle.

So that is it! That is the divine exchange, if we may reverently use that term. It is not simply, or even primarily, that God loves you, although God's agape (love) is clearly the catalyst which makes the whole thing work, but the truly good news is that Jesus will make you *right* and so present you as *righteous* before His Father. Repentance is the first essential step to becoming a Christian, and this means turning away from – turning our back upon – our old life. It certainly means a change in lifestyle, perhaps getting out of wrong relationships, perhaps giving up besetting sinful habits which are harmful to us or to others. The good news (or gospel) is an offer, not just of forgiveness (which is only the beginning) but also of *righteousness*. It is an offer to make bad people into good people, of turning sinners into saints. That is good news!

The true gospel is a double exchange. We give to Jesus our sins and He gives to us His righteousness. Plainly this is an unequal exchange: in a very real sense it is we, as repentant sinners, who are the beneficiaries of this divine transaction. It does seem, however, that many people are very happy with the thought of the *forgiveness*, and thereby what they see as the guaranteed escape from the consequences of sin, but are far less comfortable with the *righteousness* which Jesus proffers in return – that REAL change in our lives. In fact some of us do not want to accept Jesus' righteousness at all. There is that old idea of "Please God, make me holy – but not just yet"! Perhaps it is true to say that many folk want to stop at half a gospel – half a good news. We might think of God's offer in this way:

The Gospel Equation

We said earlier that it can be quite difficult to summarise the gospel, and we have suggested that some attempts by the wider church to present a gospel message that is intelligible, actually succeed only in watering it down. Your author responded to a friend via e-mail over a few weeks early in 2013, when my friend asked for a dependable statement of what it means to be a Christian, reduced to just one sentence! A good challenge, and I struggled a little bit to develop one. But in the end we settled on a form of words we both agreed seemed to 'fit the bill'! As they say colloquially, if you want to find your prince, then you have first to kiss a few frogs! In responding I prepared and then immediately eliminated some sentences that failed to 'fit the bill' adequately. Let's look at these before settling on my own favourite:

Being a Christian means to be first a disciple of Jesus, following in His footsteps and in His power, and second to be one who has made a conscious decision to follow Him as Lord (as in John 3:16).

This is part-way there. It places the primacy of Jesus first and highlights being Jesus' disciple (linked to our word "discipline"). So we are seeing Jesus as our "Master" and "Lord". But then I really need to say those things. This also hints at forgiveness, but again I have not said it.

Being a Christian means to BELIEVE in the efficacy of the cross

This is OK so far as it goes. It hints at the cross and at forgiveness, but says nothing of NEW LIFE. So it won't do. It also speaks of the "mechanics" of being "saved" but nothing of the reason.

Being a Christian means having a relationship with the Godhead through Jesus the God-Son

Again, good so far as it goes. It pulls out the RELATIONSHIP aspect, but again says nothing of new life, the Cross, etc. So, to that extent, it is inadequate.

Being a Christian means to be 'saved' from the power, the effects and the consequences of sin

Again there is some real truth in this, but WHY does God the Father save us through God the Son? Where is forgiveness – and where are the two commands that Jesus said were the MOST important i.e. to love God first (the Jewish "Shema"), and to love one's neighbour as oneself?

So, in the fullness of e-mail exchanges, we settled on the definition below. But first with a necessary explanatory note (which my friend pointed out meant I had in reality failed to achieve a one-sentence definition!). Theologically speaking, a Christian is someone who has received the Lord Jesus as Saviour (John 1:12), trusts Jesus alone for the forgiveness of sins (Acts 4:12), has put no trust in his own efforts (Isaiah 64:6) to please God, and has repented from his/her sins (Mark 1:15). So my final, one sentence working definition was this:

To be a Christian means to follow Christ, to desire Him, to fellowship with Him, to be indwelt by Him, and to bring glory to Him in your life

This definition I believe covers some of the deficiencies in the earlier attempts, if only by implication. A single sentence achieved, but assumes a certain background 'understanding', as in my explanatory note, above.

Another correspondent, this time in an online discussion forum, asked if there was a useful *gospel formula* that we can apply – some simplified way of understanding the good news of Salvation. It was perhaps the same sort of idea as my friend had – to reduce the gospel down to its essence in a reasonably intelligible way. As with the attempt at a one-sentence definition, this proved to be a difficult but, even so, a helpful exercise. Without being definitive (because in truth it is perhaps impossible to be definitive in such a simplistic way) the online group early on hit upon this, as a useful starter:

Ephesians 2:8 – **"For it is by God's grace that you have been saved through faith. It is not the result of your own efforts, but God's gift, so that no one can boast about it"**.

Therefore:

Grace + Faith = Salvation
Without Grace - no salvation
Without Faith - no salvation

Whilst this formula, *Grace + Faith = Salvation*, does not specifically draw out repentance, the cross and rebirth, they are certainly implied in the above. Salvation, said one online contributor, is BY God's grace THROUGH faith. This contributor added the following helpful clarifications:

* Grace MUST be God's definition of grace....

* Faith MUST be in Christ's death (Cross), burial, and resurrection for our sins....

* The fact that Jesus had to die to PAY the PRICE for my sins MUST lead to my repentance!

In this equation, then, we see that grace AND faith are essential for Salvation. Many people proclaim salvation is by grace, which is true. However, without the conduit of faith, we do not receive the Grace.

One New Man
Our politicians are forever telling us that peace is just around the corner. Perhaps they mean an absence of warfare between states, or between the state and terrorists. Perhaps they mean social peace through some idea of social justice, however

that might be defined. Perhaps they might be speaking of economic peace which, in its train, will bring all the other benefits and blessing that most people want: job security, a living wage, certainty about being cared for when unwell, the certainty of care when elderly. If we have learned anything in this book so far, then it should be that the absence of social ills does not necessarily lead to peace, and certainly not in that expansive and all-encompassing way suggested by the biblical concept of shalom. In our diagram of Salvation History which we explored in the previous chapter, we suggested that God has chosen a people to be His own. We suggested that God first expressed this desire for a people by choosing a people to be His special possession and to serve as a prototype and an example of what it means to live in covenant with God. God chose the Hebrew (Jewish) people, but He foreknew that they would not be totally loyal to Him, as no people-group could be totally loyal to Him. In the failings of the Hebrews was emphasised that a new and better covenant was required, and God determined to provide one. This was no surprise to God – He was not 'forced' to make alternative arrangements because of the failure of His Chosen People. No, he had always determined that covenant relationship with him would be open to all mankind.

We encounter this idea in Jeremiah 31:31. Once again readers might want to pause and review Appendix 2 which explores the relationship of the various covenants that God has "cut" with mankind.

Whilst there are a number of passages that speak into the need for Salvation and how it is obtained, the biblical account of the meeting of the Lord Jesus and the Jewish leader named Nicodemus is a compelling window into this astonishing exchange that we call "Salvation". Let us turn to look at it in detail. I have chosen the Good News translation as its English is so straightforward (John 3:1–21):

There was a Jewish leader named Nicodemus, who belonged to the party of the Pharisees. One night he went to Jesus and said to him, "Rabbi, we know that you are a teacher sent by God. No one could perform the miracles you are doing unless God were with him."

Jesus answered, "I am telling you the truth: no one can see the Kingdom of God without being born again."

"How can a grown man be born again?" Nicodemus asked. "He certainly cannot enter his mother's womb and be born a second time!"

"I am telling you the truth," replied Jesus, "that no one can enter the Kingdom of God without being born of water and the Spirit. A person is born physically of human parents, but is born spiritually of the Spirit. Do not be surprised because I tell you that you must all be born again. The wind blows wherever it wishes; you hear the sound it makes, but you do not know where it comes from or where it is going. It is like that with everyone who is born of the Spirit."

"How can this be?" asked Nicodemus.

Jesus answered, "You are a great teacher in Israel, and you don't know this? I am telling you the truth: we speak of what we know and report what we have seen, yet none of you is willing to accept our message. You do not believe me when I tell you about the things of this world; how will you ever believe me, then, when I tell you about the things of heaven? And no one has ever gone up to heaven except the Son of Man, who came down from heaven. As Moses lifted up the bronze snake on a pole in the desert, in the same way the Son of Man must be lifted up, so that everyone who believes in him may have eternal life".

For God loved the world so much that he gave his only Son, so that everyone who believes in him may not die but have eternal life. For God did not send his Son into the world to be its judge, but to be its saviour. Those

who believe in the Son are not judged; but those who do not believe have already been judged, because they have not believed in God's only Son. This is how the judgment works: the light has come into the world, but people love the darkness rather than the light, because their deeds are evil. Those who do evil things hate the light and will not come to the light, because they do not want their evil deeds to be shown up. But those who do what is true come to the light in order that the light may show that what they did was in obedience to God.

We should state at the outset that the different versions of the various modern Bible translations tend to take a different stance on where the words of Jesus and the commentary of the apostle John end and begin. In the above we have assumed that the words of Jesus end at the end of verse 15 whereas the GNB actually uses speech marks at end of verse 14. Most older translations assume Jesus' words ended at verse 14; most modern translations assume end of verse 16. Your author believes they end at verse 15, so I have taken the liberty of placing those speech marks there in the text above.

But the important point to note is that Jesus is making a clear statement about the need for new birth. This is why most Christians are quite comfortable to call themselves "born-again", marking out the key change in their life, that they are no longer their own, but rather they are now a part of God's kingdom. The radical change that has occurred in their lives is not *like* being born again, it is far more radical than that. It is a new reality, a spiritual re-birth that locates our eternal life in God's kingdom – a Kingdom in which we will invest in clear preference to this kingdom here on earth. What did Jesus say? "**Do not store up riches for yourselves here on earth, where moths and rust destroy, and robbers break in and steal. Instead, store up riches for yourselves in heaven, where moths and rust cannot destroy, and robbers cannot break in and steal. For your heart will always be where**

your riches are." (Matthew 6:19–21). Following Jesus as our Lord, becoming a part of His Kingdom, makes us His disciples. This word "disciple" locates its root in the word "discipline" – we are accepting and rejoicing in the discipline of our Lord, in whose Name we now live our lives. We are His *servants* –although *slaves* would be just as true a metaphor. No longer slaves to sin says the apostle Paul, we are slaves to righteousness. Read all of Romans chapter 6 to get a sense of what this means.

Jesus had already said (in John chapter 8) that we should not be slaves to sin. He went on, "**if the Son sets you free, you will be really free**". Jesus said this in His tense debate with the Jewish religious hierarchy, which we see recounted in John chapter 8 in its entirety. Sadly they opposed Jesus and the true peace that only He can bring. The big question for each one of us is: will we oppose Him, or will we receive Him as Lord and as Saviour?

What then is it that Jesus achieves in this new covenant which He inaugurates, that had not been achieved before? This is where it gets really interesting – indeed really exciting! What Jesus achieves is to unite two opposing men, two men who could never find peace between them, no matter how hard they tried. God in His wisdom chose a nation to be His nation of priests. This nation was the Hebrew people, elsewhere named Israel. Whilst that nation sadly failed to live out its life and be His witnesses as He required, and as they consequently earned not His honour, but instead His punishment, they nevertheless acquired a self-belief and a self-pride that set them apart from all other peoples. So we encounter the idea of "Jews and Gentiles", although it must be said that the usage of the word Gentile as expressed in most Bibles is inconsistent – and arguably incorrect.[3] There

[3] Where the context of the term is favourable, most translations use the word 'Gentile'. Where the context of the word is unfavourable, most translations use the word 'pagan'. It is rightly observed that the consistent use of the word 'pagan' would be much more correct and this in turn

was and remains a distinction between Jew and non-Jew that haunts us to this day, and tends to pit the world at large against God's chosen people. Yet God expanded His chosen people under His new covenant. So, does this worldly opposition to God's people today *include* those who are followers of Jesus? Sadly and bluntly, the answer is yes. Can believing Jew and believing Gentile be united? The answer is also yes – and Jesus has already achieved this. Let us explore what this means. We conclude this chapter with a simplistic flow-diagram that sets out the problem in a straightforward way. Readers may want to meditate on this and consider the question and answer posed below (Fig. 2).

What we are trying to represent in this simple diagram is the reality that God, as His sovereign initiative, "chooses" a nation of priests – and the world in response challenges this choice. It challenged the choice of Israel throughout the Old Testament/Promise period and it challenges that choice of a "priesthood of all believers" today. Whilst these concepts may initially be difficult for a non-Christian to fully understand, it is hoped that serious Christians will recognise the broad thrust of this argument. Indeed they may also be blessed through exploring this in a group discussion or Bible study setting.

---

raises intriguing questions about the relationship of believing Jew to believing Gentile, and what precisely it means to be a Gentile (pagan) Christian. Unfortunately full exploration of this subject is considerably beyond the scope of this book.

ONE NEW MAN –
OPPOSITION TO JEW AND TO GENTILE BELIEVER

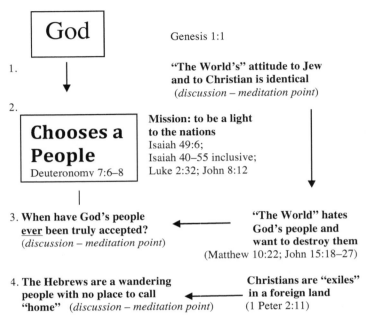

God

Genesis 1:1

1.

"The World's" attitude to Jew
and to Christian is identical
(*discussion – meditation point*)

2.

Chooses a People

Deuteronomy 7:6–8

Mission: to be a light
to the nations
Isaiah 49:6;
Isaiah 40–55 inclusive;
Luke 2:32; John 8:12

3. When have God's people
ever been truly accepted?
(*discussion – meditation point*)

"The World" hates
God's people and
want to destroy them
(Matthew 10:22; John 15:18–27)

4. The Hebrews are a wandering
people with no place to call
"home" (*discussion – meditation point*)

Christians are "exiles"
in a foreign land
(1 Peter 2:11)

Q: How can mankind be brought into a covenant relationship with a holy
God? How can there be peace between man and God?
A: By repenting and turning. By receiving Jesus as Lord and as Saviour.
By living in covenant relationship with Him.

Since Jewish people generally, and believing and active Christians specifically,
experience a parallel reality of opposition and "exile", we can recognise and
agree with the broad sentiment that these things will continue for both groups
until the realisation of the end-times prefigured in both Old Testament (the
promise) and New Testament (the promise fulfilled). God has made it plain
that, at a certain point, He will break down the dividing wall of hostility
between believing Jew and believing Gentile (Ephesians 2:16) and create One
New Man of the two.

Fig. 2

Chapter Four

ONE NEW MAN

The Eternal Search for Peace

We ended our last chapter with the thought that there is an uncomfortable reality to the age-old animosity between the world at large (and sadly this often includes elements of the "church" as well) and the Hebrew people, whom the Bible tells us that God chose to be His special ambassadors and remain forever *the apple of His eye* (Zechariah 2:8). The question of the Jewish nation and its wider relationship with the world at large and with the church in particular is a vexed one and, amongst serious Christians, one that is gaining ever greater attention. We do not want this vast subject to dominate this book on the Prince of Peace, but it is an essential backdrop and so we do need to explore it.

In our last chapter we explored the biblical theme that there is one great and awkward division within mankind, a division that God has determined to heal. That division is between Jew and non-Jew (or "Gentile"). The diagram at the end of chapter 3 introduces three linked themes:

☐ God's choice is sovereign (it is His choice and God's decisions are for all time).

☐ God works out His covenantal purposes through people – both a Chosen People and a people redeemed through a new covenant.

☐ the world at large is not in agreement with God's purposes.

The diagram posed a single question and provided an outline answer to it. Since God has already determined on a covenant-based solution to man's continuous rebellion ("sin") against Him, so we humans need to have an appreciation of how to become a part of that covenant solution. The diagram also notes (at the foot of the page) that Jews and Christians share a common experience of "exile". This is a subject, to be blunt, that is largely ignored by the broader institutional church as it tries to establish itself *within* this world and attempts to be the ambassador of Jesus. But any ambassador, almost by very nature, must be an *alien living in a foreign country*! This is a truth with which much of the institutional church seems to be thoroughly ill at ease. It is Jesus Himself who tells His followers specifically NOT to store up for ourselves treasures on earth, but rather to store our treasures in Heaven (Matthew 6:19–21). Jesus, then, invites us to have a thoroughly heaven-centred focus and ambition. In spite of the fact that much of the institutional church seems to have a decidedly worldly focus, with its preference for its idea of a social gospel, it does appear that, at long last, at the beginning of this twenty-first century, the subject of being "exiles" in a foreign land[1] is regaining the place that it had lost in the collective Christian experience, and is gaining greater recognition, as global persecution against Christians acquires ever greater momentum. The diagram at the end of chapter 3 is one to consider and meditate upon. It might also prove to be a catalyst to interesting and valuable group discussion if readers want to explore these themes with others. Let us move on.

The next point that we need to make is to state, simply and emphatically, that God recognises this sad division within mankind, between Jew and non-Jew, and He is not prepared to leave things where they stand for ever. In Ephesians 2:14 God specifically has said that He will create "one new man" out of Jew and Gentile and so will restore "peace" between them. This is achieved through the adoption as "sons" of all those who place their trust and faith in Jesus. Ephesians 2:11–22

---

[1] 1 Peter 2:11

sets this out in some detail. And elsewhere the apostle Paul records in his letter to the Roman church that the "remnant"[2] of Israel will be united – as a people chosen through grace. Here Paul seems to be saying that it is this new era of grace that will see established a new *united humanity* – a unity that will, once and for all, establish true peace under God. (See Fig. 3 and Fig. 3A below.)

Let us progress this line of thought with two further diagrams that hopefully highlight aspects of the meta-narrative we discussed in chapter 1 (see Figure 1). There has been an eternal search for peace since the beginning of time as we understand it. The Bible sets out in Genesis 3 how rebellion originally occurred and progressively establishes God's 'road map to peace' throughout the remainder of the Scriptures. We can summarise this 'road map' in our next diagram which is a summary of all that we have explored up to this point. The relationship of intimacy and trust between mankind and God was damaged and disfigured by Adam and Eve. God determined to expel them from where they were, precisely in order to initiate His divine rescue plan, involving ultimately the restoration of that intimacy – the restoration of true peace. Please spend a few minutes reviewing Fig. 3 in the next two pages. This summarises the Bible's meta-narrative in terms of Torah (sometimes called 'Law') and concludes with the truly good news that *Yeshua* (Jesus) has fulfilled Torah, so we are no longer obliged to do so. Let us be clear – the fact that *Yeshua* has fulfilled Torah/Law does not mean we are free to lead lawless lives! Perish the thought! But it does mean that if (and when?) we transgress we do have someone – yes someONE, Who can plead mercy on our behalf in the courtroom of heaven (see 1 John 2:1–6). Jesus pleads on our behalf because like us, He has lived through life's trials and temptations, yet was Himself without sin (2 Corinthians 5:21). We can fairly say, then, that Jesus is our peacemaker.

---

[2] Romans 11: 5 KJV; ONMB; NIV and various other English translations.

The Eternal Search for Peace (1)

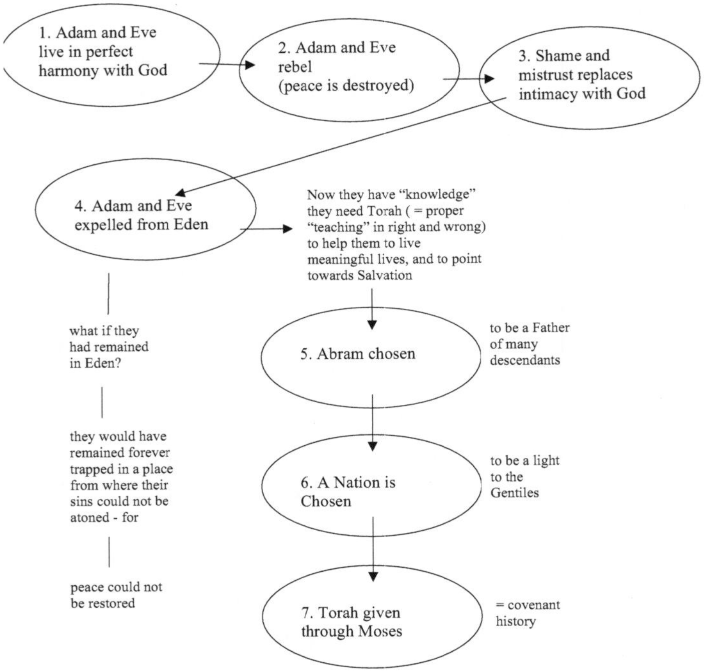

```
┌─────────────────┐      ┌─────────────────┐      ┌─────────────────┐
│ 1. Adam and Eve │      │ 2. Adam and Eve │      │ 3. Shame and    │
│ live in perfect │ ───→ │ rebel           │ ───→ │ mistrust replaces│
│ harmony with God│      │ (peace is       │      │ intimacy with God│
│                 │      │ destroyed)      │      │                 │
└─────────────────┘      └─────────────────┘      └─────────────────┘
```

┌─────────────────┐   Now they have "knowledge"
│ 4. Adam and Eve │   they need Torah (= proper
│ expelled from   │   "teaching" in right and wrong)
│ Eden   │   to help them to live
└─────────────────┘   meaningful lives, and to point
                         towards Salvation

what if they   to be a Father
had remained   ┌─────────────────┐   of many
in Eden?   │ 5. Abram chosen │   descendants
                        └─────────────────┘

they would have
remained forever
trapped in a place   ┌─────────────────┐   to be a light
from where their   │ 6. A Nation is │   to the
sins could not be   │ Chosen   │   Gentiles
atoned - for   └─────────────────┘

peace could not   ┌─────────────────┐   = covenant
be restored   │ 7. Torah given │   history
                        │ through Moses   │
                        └─────────────────┘

Torah is codified through Moses. Moses leads the children
of Israel from slavery to the promised land

Fig. 3

The Eternal Search for Peace (2)

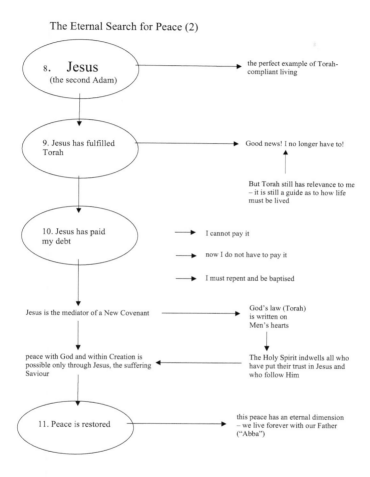

Fig. 3A

Jesus today is the mediator of the new covenant (Hebrews 9:15; 12:24) which is sealed in His blood (Matthew 26:28). Readers might again want to pause and contemplate Fig. 3 above as this sets out the problem – and the answer to the problem – in a fairly simple and straightforward way.

One New Man (2)

We return then to the problem set out in Chapter 3: there we explored briefly the idea that God is simply not prepared to leave forever the division of Jew and non-Jew. No, God has long had a plan to end this division and its associated enmity. It is frequently said, and this author believes it is fairly said, that Israel in the world today is given undeservedly an unfair and a bad press. Some Christians believe that the church is the "true Israel" because, they say, God has rejected His chosen people and instead invested His love in a *new chosen people* conveniently located within the church itself. It is difficult to sustain this argument cogently within Scripture.[3] The real situation is at once both more complex and infinitely more wonderful! God chose Israel for a purpose and He has never been frustrated in that purpose by Israel's inability (or unwillingness) to fulfil its obligations under the Moses Covenant. Refer again to Appendix 2 which sets out the key covenants – it is covenant number 3 on which we are focusing just now. In the Moses covenant God required the Hebrew nation to be a kingdom of priests *to the blessing of the entire world*. The fact that Israel floundered in its obligations and finally rejected its Messiah was never going to defeat God's Holy purposes. He had already determined to elect a priesthood of ALL believers (believers in that same Messiah – see 1 Peter 2:5) and that these believers would minister peace to the world. This priesthood of all believers would be comprised of both Jew and non-Jew, united in Messiah. And that is wonderful!

[3] A theologically "heavyweight" exploration of this question is Alex Jacobs' seminal *The Case for Enlargement Theology* – see Further Reading at the back of this book.

There is a sense in which, of course, the church might be called 'the new Israel' but it is not a term this writer would ever choose to use,[4] simply because it is a term that obscures God's ongoing purposes for the Jewish people in this world. Indeed the idea has been used by parts of the church as a convenient cover story for the church's own recurrent bouts of persecution against the Jews, culminating today– in the twenty-first century – in the institutional church's determined project to create within the heart of national Israel (*Eretz Israel*) a Palestinian "homeland" that would simultaneously pepper its geographical integrity and act as a potential dagger at its heart as a political state. So how, then, might the church legitimately be called 'Israel'? Only in the remote sense that it is grafted in to the root stock that is Israel[5] and it speaks today as ambassadors for Jesus the Messiah. The good news here is that more and more Jewish people are also coming to recognise Jesus as Messiah, so the "voice" of the ambassadors of Jesus is no longer solely a Gentile (non-Jewish) one.

This book does not seek to provide an answer the current difficulties of the Middle East, nor to explore the sad reality of what has become known as the "Palestinian problem". It is useful, however, to consider Israel as a mirror, in terms of its relationship both with the institutional church and with all people as individuals. Again we do not want to make too much of this subject as it takes us away from our central theme of The Prince of Peace. But Figure 4 outlines this by suggesting that in Israel we can detect a counterpoint mirror image reflecting both the institutional church and you and me as individuals! The sad truth of the Old Testament/Tanakh/ Promise is that Israel *the chosen ethnic nation* rebelled against God specifically by failing to fulfil its covenant obligations. In yet other ways Israel sinned against God by its persistent failure to care for the vulnerable in society (often cited as widows, orphans and aliens). And specifically it forgot or

---

[4] Note this misleading term is found nowhere in Scripture.

[5] Romans 11:17 in particular, but all of Romans chapter 11 is relevant.

ignored its duty to worship but one God – the true God – and instead continually chased after false pagan "gods". This led eventually to national disaster.

But what of the institutional church? Does it mirror the experience and the record of Old Testament Israel? The church has rebelled against God in all sorts of ways. The church is

Israel as a Mirror

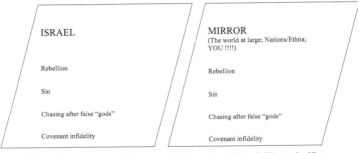

This is why we can recognize so much of ourselves in Israel. We can be like Israel in attitudes and actions. Israel is a prototype of all other Nations. Israel is a prototype of YOU !!!

Fig. 4

as guilty of sin as biblical Israel. Can anyone name a sin that Israel committed that the institutional church has not also committed? And what of you, dear reader? Have you rebelled against God's right to be your Master? Have you sinned? Have you chased after false gods? There are many false gods – not just the ones that are sometimes referred to as the "Babylon Mystery" gods. What about the idolisation of sports, or politics, or "celebrities". What about the idolisation of money, or power, or sex? Have we been covenantally faithful – even those of us who claim to follow Jesus the Messiah? If God's law is summarised in the Ten Commandments, how many of these Commandments have each of us actually broken? If Israel failed (and it did) then we have also, each and every one of us, failed. Readers might want to reflect on Figure 4 for a few moments before proceeding.

True peace, true shalom, is possible in this world and the next. The remainder of this book seeks to explore that wonderful theme. Before we leave this promise of *one new man*, and God's holy project to create one new man out of two, let us reconsider for a moment the bigger picture of God's Salvation purposes. In chapter 2 we looked in diagram form at the meta-narrative of scripture, at God's big-picture plan to rescue mankind from the grip, the power and the consequences of sin. God's plan, we might say, was always a two-pronged attack on the question. Always, from the very beginning, it involved a man.[6] That man would be THE Saviour, who would ultimately usher-in a new age, the age of grace. The themes we set out in Fig. 1 show, in outline, that a national chosen people would, in time, become a global chosen people that will live in covenantal relationship with God. And this relationship will be one of peace and harmony, extending into eternity.

It will be helpful now to place some biblical authority on these claims. Some readers may complain that there is no division between Jew and Gentile, and that, as far as they are concerned, Jewish people are just like everyone else. Of course at a superficial level this is true. Both Jew and Gentile search for peace and need peace. Culturally, Jews are today not a million miles away from other people groups – and the Jewish faith, through Christianity, has influenced the entire world, especially in the development of the concept of democracy. Are Jew and non-Jew so very different? This is a big and deep subject that we will not adequately plumb in this short book. But we can make some helpful generalisations. The Bible certainly draws out a clear distinction between the Hebrew nation and the other nations. The supporting biblical texts in Figure 2 (chapter 3) show that God's people were called to be separate and God's laws in terms of restricting intermarriage with other "nations" (and that meant pagan

---

[6] Christian theologians generally state that Genesis 3:15 is the first direct allusion to Jesus the Messiah.

nations!) were designed to keep the Hebrew nation pure. A dividing wall was established between the Hebrews and everyone else. There is no reason to believe this was not in God's foreknowledge, even if it was not in God's ultimate plan. That division would need to be ended at a certain point in time and God determined to end it in and through the man *Yeshua* (Jesus). At this point it is important to affirm openly that 'Jesus' is in fact not the Lord's actual Name, surprising and alarming though this may be to some readers! "Jesus" is only the English translation of the Latin translation of the Greek translation of His Hebrew name, which is *Yeshua*. Just how important this is, is not for us to explore in this book.[7]

We can also affirm that the mechanism to bring each individual person into right relationship with God is identical for Jew and for Gentile. Once again we can best express this in diagram format, with supporting biblical texts. The first thing to say is that for both Jew and non-Jew, *the requirement remains to respond to the offer of life extended by God the Father*. We explored a little of this needed response in chapter 3. Biblically we can demonstrate the relationship of *one new man*. Please refer now to Figure 5 below. Ideally a diligent and systematic review of the supporting biblical texts will help to consolidate this line of thought. If readers want to do this then they should set aside sufficient time (an evening?). But the simple truth is that *the journey to peace for both Jew and non-Jew is identical*, even if they might commence their journeys from slightly different starting points. It is a *restored humanity* that God intends to create – a "nation" of those who have placed their trust in Jesus the Messiah (*Yeshua ha Mashiach*).

Our diagram shows quite simply that the unbeliever must first recognise their own sin (rebellion against God) and see it as a deadly serious problem that needs to be resolved.

---

[7] The various books of UK writer Steve Maltz help us to explore some of this. See Further Reading section at the back of this book for some suggestions.

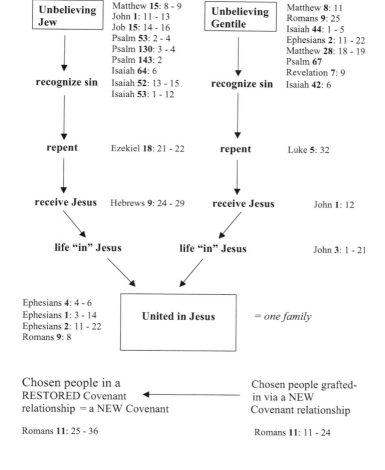

Fig. 5

Indeed a deadly serious disease that needs to be healed! This recognition is something considerably beyond a mere mental assent ("I'm a bit bad and I'd like to be a bit better!"). It is a heartfelt realisation and the sinner recognises and understands that, in some way upon which they find it difficult to focus, if their sins are left untreated, then this will lead to disaster, indeed to spiritual death itself. Repentance (a genuine turning-away) from sin follows, together with the conscious and serious decision to receive *Yeshua* (Jesus) as Lord and as Saviour. It is "in" Him[8] that we find our unified life within a global family of believers. And it is within this family that we find true peace.

Horizontal or Vertical?
As we will see later in this book, Jesus does not promise peace for His followers in this world. If anything, the suggestion is rather the reverse; that choosing to follow Him (to be His disciple) is likely to bring you into conflict with the power structures of this world – sooner or later. This is not something to be frightened about as God will have the final say, but we need to be realistic about the pervasiveness of opposition, and that such opposition entails a cost to us.

So what can we say definitively about the joys of discipleship in Jesus?

☐ To be a follower of Jesus will entail the joyful outcome that you have a new family and new friends

Christian people are not perfect. But in their company we can often find an extraordinary unity of spirit – indeed a peace – that passes all human understanding.

---

[8] A fascinating additional investigation for the diligent student: see how many times the New Testament book of Ephesians tells us that we are to be found "in" Jesus. Your author counted at least 16 references in this medium-length letter to the Ephesian church (NIV translation).

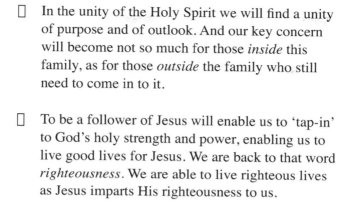

☐ In the unity of the Holy Spirit we will find a unity of purpose and of outlook. And our key concern will become not so much for those *inside* this family, as for those *outside* the family who still need to come in to it.

☐ To be a follower of Jesus will enable us to 'tap-in' to God's holy strength and power, enabling us to live good lives for Jesus. We are back to that word *righteousness*. We are able to live righteous lives as Jesus imparts His righteousness to us.

There will be many other joyful realities to being a part of God's Kingdom, but hopefully the above has suggested that we can find harmonious relationships within this *Kingdom people*. And we can assert this in spite of the reality that too often the churches seem to be riven with difficulties and dissensions. Apart from whatever this may suggest about our own weaknesses as humans, it perhaps also suggests that Christians face an active and clever spiritual enemy, who is out to fight the church at every opportunity.

We can say then, that the first and most profound reality of new life in Jesus is that the *vertical relationship*, between man and God, is restored. God Himself adopts us to be a part of His family and we can enjoy real intimacy with God as He dwells in us. This is an amazing claim to make. It can only be said that the real life experience of millions upon millions of Christian believers across this world shows that this is a reality. Truly we can cry out joyfully "Abba" – Father, and affirm that He enters truly and profoundly into our lives. This is re-birth!

What about the horizontal relationship – between people? Is this fully restored? Certainly Christians find it possible to live in situations that are deeply challenging. We find that, in spite of difficulties, we can learn to forgive and that this forgiveness is a reality. Why do we forgive? Why MUST we forgive? We must forgive because whatever wrongs we may have suffered at the hands of others, they are unlikely to be worse than the wrongs that Jesus willingly suffered, particularly that, being sinless Himself, He willingly accepted the punishment that should justly have been ours to bear. We must forgive because Jesus told us to forgive (Matthew 18:21–35). Also in the Lord's prayer He taught us: "Father... forgive us as we have forgiven others" – Matthew 6:9–13. Our agape (love) is to go beyond forgiveness, important though this is. We are to show love to our enemies[9] and resist the desire to judge others by standards that we may not ourselves be prepared to observe. As Jesus said, we are to be born again, and it is only this true new birth that enables us to live lives that truly meet these high ethical and moral standards.

So, we must affirm that it is the vertical relationship that primarily is restored and magnified by faith in *Yeshua* (Jesus). Our relationship with God becomes one of increasing unity of outlook and purpose as we progressively grow more like our heavenly Father – our Abba. Our horizontal relationships should also be impacted positively by this new and restored vertical axis, but as we are inevitably involved with others who do not know – or indeed have actively rejected – Jesus, so it may be more difficult to live peaceably on the horizontal axis, especially as the desire to live in shalom may be one-sided.

And yet within the body of believers peace is a hallmark. A brief look at the Gospel of Luke helps us to recognise God's intention to bring peace – shalom – as a substitute for Ra, that chaos and anarchy which we met in chapter 2. So what does Luke teach us about peace?

Luke 1:79 As the old priest Zechariah prophesies following his own son's birth, his own son being John who we all know and remember as "John the Baptist", Zechariah goes on to

---

[9] Note we are not called to like our enemies!

rejoice at the prospect of THE Saviour Who will "guide our steps into the path of peace". The whole of Zechariah's prophesy has the heady scent of Salvation about it (see Luke 1:67–79). ⬜ This salvation will bring in its train a profound peace. Zechariah's prophecy seems to combine both the vertical and horizontal dimensions to peace.

Luke 2:14 As the angels sing out the wondrous truth of a Saviour born in Bethlehem, they affirm God's intention to bring "peace on earth" through the new-born Saviour. But this peace on earth is not, as most of our Christmas cards misquote it, "peace on earth and goodwill to all men". No, this is "peace on earth to those with whom He is pleased". God does not lavish His peace willy-nilly on all people. No, He lavishes it upon those on whom His favour rests. It is difficult to reach any other conclusion except that this peace ultimately "rests" upon those who have placed their trust in the shed blood of God's dear Son, and upon His finished work on the cross of crucifixion.

Luke 10:6 As Jesus sends out 72 disciples to preach the good news of Jesus' imminent arrival, acting as His heralds or forerunners, so Jesus tells them (v. 5) "Whenever you go into a house, first say shalom be with this house". And Jesus continues in v. 6 "if a shalom-loving man lives there, let your greeting of peace remain upon him; if not take back your greeting of shalom." This is challenging and uncomfortable to us, but it seems to recognise the sad reality that not all will be willing to accept the good news of peace. We are not, then, to overstay our welcome. Jesus elsewhere says "do not cast pearls before swine" (Matthew 7:6) which might be understood in this way: where people belittle the message of good news or belittle the Word of God, then do not go on offering them these good things. They must then stand or fall by their own efforts. If peace is specifically rejected by those who refuse Jesus, then we must at some point, and prompted by the Holy Spirit, simply move on. Others will listen, so we are not to waste time pursuing the determinedly lost.

Luke 12:51 This is perhaps the most uncomfortable saying of Jesus and we must recognise it for what it is. Jesus is not, as He is too often portrayed, "gentle Jesus, meek and mild". (Your author does not know how this specific epithet is derived, nor who first said it!). No, Jesus is the only person who can bring peace between man and God – that vertical relationship. As Jesus headed resolutely away from Galilee, where He had ministered, to Jerusalem, where He would be judicially murdered by the Roman occupiers and their local lackies, the Temple priesthood, Jesus knew that time was running out and that He would need to speak ever more directly:

> **"I came to set the earth on fire, and how I wish it were already kindled! I have a baptism to receive, and how distressed I am until it is over! Do you suppose that I came to bring peace to the world? No, not peace, but division. From now on a family of five will be divided, three against two and two against three. Fathers will be against their sons, and sons against their fathers; mothers will be against their daughters, and daughters against their mothers; mothers-in-law will be against their daughters-in-law, and daughters-in-law against their mothers-in-law"** (Luke 12:49–53).

Plainly this is not shalom as we recognise it. What is Jesus saying? There is a sad reality, that those who place their faith in Jesus, and especially those who are baptised into His name and into His family, will themselves make others – those outside the fold – feel desperately uncomfortable. They will sense that the true Christian has something that they do not have, and simultaneously they must be both jealous and fearful. Jealous that they do not have that something (or someONE) who could be beneficial to them but yet whom they do not want, and fearful that in this rejection, they will face an inevitable consequence. And the constant reminder of this consequence is the presence amongst them of those who are disciples of *Yeshua* (Jesus). So, as Jesus says, there will be family divisions. There can scarcely be a Christian on the face of this planet who has not experienced first-hand these familial tensions. No, Jesus did not come to bring an easy peace – not peace at any price. Jesus came to bring a costly peace that divides. Jesus was distressed (v. 50) as He knew the appalling cost that would be His to bear, in securing eternal peace for us, people who are sinners and who need to be saved.

Luke 14:32 Here Jesus reminds His followers that there is a cost-calculation to be made: we have already said *Yeshua* did not come to bring peace at any price. And we have to weigh the cost of choosing to follow Him. *Yeshua* used three metaphors of this cost (see Luke 14:25–33). We focus now upon the last:

"If a king goes out with ten thousand men to fight another king who comes against him with twenty thousand men, he will sit down first and decide if he is strong enough to face that other king. If he isn't, he will send messengers to meet the other king to ask for terms of peace while he is still a long way off. In the same way," concluded Jesus, "none of you can be my disciple unless you give up everything you have."

(Luke 14:31–33)

This is truly uncomfortable! Jesus does not ask for a little bit of us to follow Him. He does not ask for our Sunday observance, leaving Monday to Saturday as our private playground. No, Jesus demands our all, just as He has given us His all. What Jesus gave will always be immeasurably greater that what we might be asked to give. But, nevertheless, a cool calculation is to be made. If we purport to follow Him, we must live TOTALLY by His standards; we do not pick and choose which bits of His revelation to accept and then argue about the rest. Make that calculation. The author's mother (Violet Ruth Sammons) once commented, "The Christian way of life is the hardest way that this world offers." Now this comment should be fully explored in the light of Jesus' own statement in Matthew 11:30 (readers are invited to look it up!). There is more than a grain of truth in my mother's comment, however. The ethical standards by which a true Christian is called to live are absolutely without parallel. The commitment is to be total. Failure in the Christian life brings dishonour on *Yeshua* and almost serves to place Him back upon the cross (see Hebrews 6:6).

Luke 19:38 The backdrop here is the triumphant entry into Jerusalem, just hours before the Lord's passion and crucifixion. Here in this excited, possibly frenzied scene we see someone in the crowd excitedly recognising *Yeshua* for who He actually is, whether or not this nameless person truly understood the full implications of what He was saying. This man lauded Jesus, calling Him "the King" who comes in the name of the Lord. And on top of this he excitedly says "peace in heaven and glory to God". In response, the self-appointed religious leaders of the Jerusalem Temple show their profound distaste for what is going on. They do not like the term 'King'. Firstly, it might upset their Roman overlords (political implications) and secondly, they are themselves completely and irreversibly unwilling to bow the knee to this new King (theological implications). They tell Jesus, in effect, to tell His followers to 'shut-up', in modern parlance. Jesus does not argue the point with them, however. He simply dismisses it as irrelevant – see v. 40!

So it is that King Jesus brings peace to this world. He brings peace in the vertical dimension as well as in the horizontal dimension. But He also causes division. Matthew

10:34 perhaps summarises this perfectly, in another difficult saying of Jesus. This is in fact a repetition of what Luke has recorded in Luke 12. Matthew records it slightly differently:

"Those who declare publicly that they belong to me, I will do the same for them before my Father in heaven. But those who reject me publicly, I will reject before my Father in heaven. Do not think that I have come to bring peace to the world. No, I did not come to bring peace, but a sword. I came to set sons against their fathers, daughters against their mothers, daughters-in-law against their mothers-in-law (Matthew 10:32–35).

Let us ignore the family dimension to this for a moment. *Yeshua* did not come to bring pace but a sword. Where Jesus is encountered, strong emotions must ensue, either in love and dedication to Him, or in hard or soft rebellion against Him. There is no middle ground.

His mother Miriam (Mary) also would encounter the "sword" of which Jesus spoke. The aged God-fearer Simeon, who we read about in Matthew 2, in giving praise to God for the safe delivery of the infant Jesus, was very direct with Mary. He prophesied that "sorrow, like a sharp sword" would "break" her heart. For some the joy of finding peace with God through Jesus His Son, will need to be weighed against the reality that Jesus' presence tends to divide and that friendships – and even family relationships – can be severely dislocated by a decision to become His true disciple. How many are there in the world today, who have "lost" their family, following the decision to follow Jesus? And how many down through history? There IS a profound cost to following Jesus – and He has been open and honest about it. But the peace that follows that good decision is a peace that is more than compensatory. It is a peace that enables us to live for Him. It is a peace that, on occasions, enables us to die for Him too. It is a reality that two who are profoundly set apart can become *One New*

Man to the Glory of God. This is no cheap peace. It is not peace at any price.

Chapter Five

GOOD NEWS!

Human Rights and Human Wrongs

So far in this book we have taken an in-depth look at what the Bible says about peace – that true shalom that God desires to give to us. We have also focused on what it means to be a disciple of *Yeshua* (Jesus) and seen that His mission, and His ministry, was one of ultimate peace-making, in both the vertical and horizontal dimensions. Vertical and horizontal: a cross of peace? A cross of love? It is sometimes said that the Bible, just like the other religious writings, contains bellicosity which some people have used as a means to "justify" warfare and even terrorism. Your author considers this to be seriously faulty reasoning, however. As we saw in Chapter 2, the Bible contains a definite meta-narrative, an overall story with a distinct "shape" to it – it is the story of Salvation. The story of Salvation has a defined beginning, a middle and a clear end in view. The same cannot be claimed of the other religious writings. The Koran of Islam, for example, does not contain a meta-narrative and its instructions on war and on peace have to be understood in Mohammad's life in his Meccan and Medinan periods, respectively. In Mecca he enjoyed a measure of acceptance and his writings have a more pacific vein. After expulsion from Mecca his writings became more warlike. It is interesting that this clear distinction is not recognised or even alluded to in most western RE[1] teaching materials (review for example the UK BBC's "bite-size"

---

[1] Religious education

religious education on the internet). The concept of abrogation must be applied to the Koranic writings, and Muslims have no unified view of how abrogation works in practice. Similar observations might be made about the other religious writings.

Is it even-handed, then, to say that the Bible has no equivalence to the bellicosity of other religious writings? What about the so-called "violent" verses in the Bible? As we said in Chapter 1, any verse should be examined in its context. Remember the old adage "a verse taken out of context is a pretext". It is true that some biblical verses have on occasions been used out of context in this way but this is, in fact, extremely rare in practice. If readers doubt this then they might want to see if they can readily identify perhaps three specific occasions when a verse from the Bible has been used as a 'justification' for some violent act or violent attitude. Your author suspects they will have considerable difficulty in doing so. If readers want to explore this subject in a little more detail, then they might want to read *The Empty Promise of Godism*[2] and in particular Chapter 3 which looks at some of the supposedly difficult elements of the Bible and finds that, where they exist, they are NOT capable of being used as a precedent for bellicosity today. Furthermore, in research on the Crusades (which seem to have had geopolitical rather than religious imprimatur), your author has been unable to find any examples of the religious or political leaders of the day specifically appealing to Scripture to "justify" their Crusades. Rather, an early just war theorem appears to have been applied, with the generic assumption that God would be very much "behind" the effort of liberation of the Holy Land from Muslim occupation. That the offer of forgiveness for past sins was available as a 'reward' to Crusaders for participation seems to be factual, but no Scripture would support such an idea. The oft-heard argument that the Crusades were based on biblical justifications is, in fact, an urban myth.

---

[2] At time of writing, this book is freely available chapter by chapter as PDFs. Just Google the Glory to Glory Publications' website.

We can only repeat, then, that the Bible is the story of Salvation, and its major "deliverable", if we can put it so prosaically, is true shalom – true peace along vertical and horizontal axes. Our modern society is very fond of the idea of human rights, as they believe that enshrining these "rights" into law leads to more "fairness" and so to greater peace. What did Jesus say about human rights and what does the Bible say about human rights? Jesus' specific teachings are encompassed throughout the four Gospels (Matthew, Mark, Luke and John). Matthew 5–7 inclusive are called 'the sermon on the mount' and encompass much of His ethical and moral instruction. It is notable that in the so-called 'beatitudes' (Matthew 5:3–11) Jesus goes out of His way to turn the world's ideas upside down. The peace bestowed by Jesus is certainly not as the world recognises it. It is not until the very end of His ministry that Jesus specifically offers His peace to His disciples. What did He say?

It is in the context of the promise of the Holy Spirit that the Lord makes His gift known. As Jesus knows that He is about to be taken from the disciples, indeed taken from this world, He promises them a "Helper", someONE Who will dwell in believers, empowering them with Jesus' holiness.

"Peace is what I leave with you; it is my own peace that I give you. I do not give it as the world does. Do not be worried and upset; do not be afraid. You heard me say to you, 'I am leaving, but I will come back to you.' If you loved me, you would be glad that I am going to the Father; for he is greater than I. I have told you this now before it all happens, so that when it does happen, you will believe. I cannot talk with you much longer, because the ruler of this world is coming. He has no power over me, but the world must know that I love the Father; that is why I do everything as he commands me" (John 14:27–31).

Shortly afterwards, in what would be, prior to the crucifixion, His final discourse with His disciples, Jesus says "I have told you this so that you will have peace by being united to me. The world will make you suffer. But be brave! I have defeated the world!" (John 16:33). Jesus has left His peace. Whilst He gave peace to so many to whom He ministered in Galilee and Judea, a real peace through healing and a real peace through the assurance of sins forgiven, Jesus would leave HIS peace for all time to those who place their faith in Him. It is a peace that sustains us through times of trouble. Elsewhere Jesus warned, **"If the world hates you, just remember that it has hated me first"** (John 15:18). To follow *Yeshua* involves a certain "cost" in terms of conflict with this world.

Any open-minded exploration of the whole Bible leaves us reasonably certain that man, as God's special creation, is endowed by God with certain "human rights". A diligent student of the Bible will be encouraged toward ideals such as equity and justice. The founding fathers of the USA put it well: "all men are created equal . . . endowed by their Creator with certain unalienable rights." This accords with Scripture. The Bible says that mankind is created in the image of God (Genesis 1:27). Because of this, man has a special dignity and has been given dominion over the rest of creation (Genesis 1:26). The Mosaic Law is replete with examples of how God expects people to be treated humanely. The Ten Commandments contain prohibitions against murder, theft, coveting, adultery, and bearing false testimony. Other examples in the Torah (teaching) include commands to treat immigrants well (Exodus 22:21; Leviticus 19:33–34), to provide for the poor (Leviticus 19:10; Deuteronomy 15:7–8), to grant interest-free loans to the poor (Exodus 22:25), and to release all indentured servants every fifty years (Leviticus 25:39–41).

The Bible teaches that God does not show favouritism (Acts 10:34). Every person is a unique creation of His, and

He loved each one (see John 3:16; 2 Peter 3:9). **"Rich and poor have this in common: The LORD is the Maker of them all"** (Proverbs 22:2). In turn, the Bible teaches that Christians should not discriminate based on race, gender, cultural background or social standing (Galatians 3:28; Colossians 3:11; James 2:1–4). We are to be kind to all (Luke 6:35–36). The Bible gives strict warnings against taking advantage of the poor and downtrodden. **"He who oppresses the poor shows contempt for their Maker, but whoever is kind to the needy honours God"** (Proverbs 14:31). Rather, God's people are to help whoever is in need (Proverbs 14:21; Matthew 5:42; Luke 10:30–37). Most Christians down through the ages have understood their responsibility to assist their fellow human beings. The majority of hospitals and orphanages in our world – certainly the early ones – were founded by concerned Christians. Many of the great humanitarian reforms of history, including abolition of slavery, were spearheaded by Christians seeking justice for all made in the image of God. Today, Christians are still working hard to relieve human rights abuses and to promote the welfare of all people. As they preach the good news of peace around the world, they are also digging wells, planting crops, dispensing medicine, giving clothes and providing education for the poor and destitute. This is as *Yeshua* requires. We do this to honour Him, as well as being an act of agape love towards others. Interestingly, some Jewish aid organisations also work selflessly and without recognition for similar ends, even in regions ill-disposed towards Israel.

So, does the Bible specifically highlight any "right" that is inalienable to all mankind? Immediately we must state that there is a sense in which a Christian believer has no "rights" of their own, because they have surrendered their life to the Messiah. Messiah "owns" the believer. **"You are not your own; you were bought at a price"** (1 Corinthians 6:19–20). But God's authority over us does not diminish God's image in us. Our submission to the will of God certainly does not abrogate God's command to love our neighbour as ourselves (Matthew 23:39). In fact, we serve God most when we serve others (Matthew 25:40). Yet the Bible does state specifically ONE right that we must acknowledge as being a right given to ALL humans. It is found in John 1:12. Let us see the context:

The Word was in the world, and though God made the world through him, yet the world did not recognize him. He came to his own country, but his own people did not receive him. Some, however, did receive him and believed in him; so he gave them the right to become God's children. They did not become God's children by natural means, that is, by being born as the children of a human father; God himself was their Father.

This, then, is THE inalienable human right – the right to be a member of God's family. There is no power on earth or in the heavenlies that can take that right away from any person. No government can take that right away. No religion can take that right away. Yet this gift of life is not automatic. The gift of entry into His family is a gift that must be accepted. In legal contractual terms (and your author has spent much of his career writing contracts!) the "offer" must be "unequivocally accepted". The "consideration", or price paid, is literally the Blood of Jesus, as we saw in chapter 3. What wonderful peace it should bring to every person on this planet, that each one has THAT right, given directly by God Himself. How do we close with this new covenant promise? It is as easy as ABC, as someone once said:

We need to **admit** our need of forgiveness – and that in turn means admitting we are in fact sinners. Jesus confirmed that sin is the barrier that prevents us from peace with God. The Bible is certain that we are all sinners (Romans 3:23).

We need to **believe** in Jesus and what He has achieved for us. He alone was sinless so he alone can pay the price of sin – the debt that we owe to God for our sins, and which we cannot pay.

We need to receive Him and **commit** our lives to Him, becoming His faithful followers (or disciples). The demonstration of commitment is usually accompanied by believer's baptism, that act of saying to the world at large that I now belong to Jesus.

Admit + Believe + Commit = Life = Peace

or

A + B + C = L / P

God really has made this very simple for us! Some people might say that Jesus did not major on the reality of sin. A simple Google search, however, "what did Jesus say about sin" may help people to see that in fact *Yeshua* did refer to the tragedy of sin often. In brief: *Yeshua* (Jesus) taught about the nature of sin itself. Sin, said *Yeshua*, is a master to whom we become enslaved (John 8:34). Only the truth will set us free (John 8:32). Sin is blinding (John 9:39–41). The conscience's reprimands are harder to hear the more we persist in sin (cf. Hebrews 3:12–13). Positive influences and opportunities are removed when we disregard the longsuffering and goodness of God (cf. Luke 8:12; Romans 1:20, 21, 24, 26, 28; 2:4–5). Only humble submission and sincere obedience to Jesus Christ will remedy our spiritual blindness.

Jesus also taught that the remedy to sin was His ultimate mission. The Lord said to the paralysed man, "Your sins are forgiven" (Luke 5:20). Subsequently, *Yeshua* healed the man to prove His divine right to forgive sins. Similarly, He instructed Simon the Pharisee when he said, "I tell you, then, the great love she has shown proves that her many sins have been forgiven. But whoever has been forgiven little shows only a little love." Then Jesus said to the woman, "Your sins are forgiven." [Greek perfect tense; i.e., were forgiven and remain forgiven]" (Luke 7:47–48). When the Lord was criticised for eating with sinners, He confirmed the purpose of His mission by responding, **"People who are well do not**

need a doctor, but only those who are sick. I have not come to call respectable people to repent, but sinners." (Luke 5:31–32).

It is your right! It is your right to become a child of God! What does this mean in practice? This is a huge subject which we cannot fully explore here. But in essence it means that you are adopted into God's family and so have 'inheritance rights' in that family – the right to be with your Father forevermore. A share, if you like, in His Kingdom throughout eternity. That is wonderful because God is a Father who truly loves and He has demonstrated that love for us (Romans 5:8). I will recommend that readers pause here and read Romans 5:1–11 as this opens up the subject a little. ⬜

(Romans 8:14 and 1 John 3:2 also speak into this).

The Jesus Factor

It must be said that true, biblical Christianity is not a religion in the same sense as the other major religions (nor indeed the many thousands of minor religions). Jesus (*Yeshua*) promises us His peace, but He never promises material prosperity nor a life of ease. Both these things may indeed come to a true believer, and it is an observable fact that over time, individual Christians and Christian communities do seem to prosper – not in any outlandish way, but we rightly anticipate that God will bless our efforts as we live as His children. However we are to make our principal investments, our spiritual investments, in heaven – not here on earth – and heaven is where our heart should be. *Yeshua* at one point invited His disciples (and that is all who place their trust in Him) to pick up their cross daily and to follow Him (Luke 9:23). He did not tell us to pick up our cushions and slippers! The symbol He told us to take up is the cross – a symbol of death.

It is not the purpose of this book to explore differences between the religions. In my earlier book *The Empty Promise of Godism* I did explore a few of the glaring and irreconcilable differences between the religions in Chapter Six. If readers really want to explore this spiritual cul-de-sac then, by all means, check out that chapter as it may be useful – and it remains freely available via the Glory to Glory Publications' website in PDF format. However I will suggest here that true biblical Christianity gives a reality of peace and of certainty that the various religions do not, and cannot. The religions, generally speaking, tell their adherents that they must observe certain religious practices. Whilst these may be culturally relevant, and to that extent deliver a measure of cultural peace with their religious neighbours, they still leave the sinner – and that is all of us – dead in our sins and ultimately facing judgement. The wonderful shalom and assurance of salvation is absent. Instead there is the uneasy certainty that judgement must still be faced. Unease at the prospect of the future is what the various religions seem to deliver, not the certainty of eternal relationship with a loving Father.

As the risk of over-simplifying this matter, we can perhaps see the topography of the question in the simple diagram below, headed The Jesus Factor. Why would I choose a religion when *Yeshua* simply calls me to follow Him and to learn from Him? He offers a relationship, not a legal system! Take a look at Fig. 6.

I repeat that this is somewhat simplified but hopefully readers will see within this simplicity a profound truth. Let us finish this chapter with a key passage on relationship through *Yeshua*. As the passage is a long one, readers will need to read it in a Bible. I will highlight just one verse for a double-take: Act 10:36, but this is right in the middle of the passage which is all of Acts chapter 10. Let me just set the scene: Saul of Tarsus, who has been persecuting the believers, hounding them and approving of their religious execution as a punishment for following *Yeshua*, has himself been confronted by that same *Yeshua* (see Acts 9). Saul (later Paul) has become a disciple. In the next chapter (10), Peter, the disciple of *Yeshua* who had denied *Yeshua* three times

THE PRINCE OF PEACE

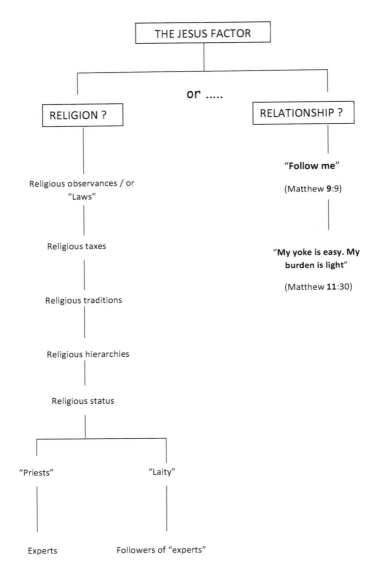

Fig. 6

before the crucifixion, is now a recognised leader of the early church. He still, however, is "locked-in" to the thought of the Moses covenant, and feels that in order to be proper disciples of *Yeshua*, people must also adopt the religious practices of the Hebrews. He has not yet really understood the amazing truth of one new man, Jew and non-Jew united in Messiah, living as family together.

God now confronts Peter by telling him, in a vision, to eat "unclean" (non-kosher) food – which Peter at first rejects. Then God arranges for Peter to meet Cornelius – a non-Jew who has become a true believer. Finally Peter understands the message. Disciples of Jesus do not need to become Jewish in order to live aright – they need instead to follow Him faithfully and in accordance with the simple rules that Jesus has set out. The shalom that passes all understanding is for Jew and non-Jew alike.

No new religion here, just a relationship of trust, love and faithful service, as we live in *Yeshua* our Lord and Saviour, trusting in His righteousness not our own. Now that is good news!

Please read Acts Chapter 10.

Chapter Six

THE CITY OF PEACE

What did Jesus say about peace and war?
We have already seen that Jesus was quite clear that the peace which He brings is not as the world understands that word. Indeed He went further, and affirmed that there will be wars and rumours of wars until the end of time. Where and when did He say this and what was the context?

The context first: after *Yeshua's* triumphant entry to Jerusalem, and after He had cleared the temple of the traders, He began the final phase of His teaching which had a definite eschatological ("end times") focus. *Yeshua* knew that He was about to be crucified, becoming THE Passover Lamb for all time and for all people – the Lamb that takes away the sins of the world (John 1:29). There was not much time left; so much to say, and so little time in which to say it. His disciples (and this includes you and me) need to know the rough 'topography' of what lies ahead. Jesus provides this in Matthew 24 through 25. (See also Mark 13, Luke 21:5–36 and, in a certain way, John 17). ⬛

Each of these speaks both of the immediate future and of the longer-term eschatological outworking of God's purposes. It is well beyond the scope of this book to explore biblical eschatology in detail – indeed there are a number of competing and mutually exclusive ideas. What we *can* say with assurance is that:

- Jesus will return
- We are given prophecies about the future in which the world becomes more and more at odds with itself, and with God – the God of Abraham, Isaac and Jacob.

At this point I will encourage the diligent reader to stop and read each of those passages mentioned above. There is no way that I can put this more succinctly or more cogently than the Scriptures themselves and ... YOU NEED TO KNOW! The Holy Spirit would not have provided this information if it was unimportant. Indeed there is a simple, practical, element to this as well. Since believers are going to live through troubled times (that is what the word "tribulation" means) we need to know that God has not lost control, so we do not give up on our faith.

Where did Jesus give this teaching? In Jerusalem. To whom did He provide it? Directly, to the immediate core group of disciples, those whom He had already called. Indirectly, He is giving it to me and to you! *The future is important* and we need to be prepared for it. As He tells the disciples about the "signs" of the end of the age, He tells us specifically that warfare will never be absent. Three verses in Matthew chapter 24 must be kept at the forefront of our minds:

"**Watch out that no one deceives you. For many will come in my name, claiming, 'I am the Christ', and will deceive many. You will hear of wars and rumours of wars, but see to it that you are not alarmed. Such things must happen, but the end is still to come**" (Matthew 24:4–6, NIV).

Deception is something we must always be aware of, and alert to. It is not just a few that will come in the name of "Jesus" to spread false teaching. No, says Jesus, it is "many". We need forever to be alert to what the institutional church is "teaching" and what their associated "theologians" are "discovering" in the Bible. How many theologians and clerics today teach concepts that run directly counter to the clear demands of Scripture? Is this, indeed, a "sign of the times"?[1] It is even true that some men will arise claiming to be *the* Messiah (or Christ). Although we have not yet seen this in the institutional church, we have certainly seen it in some of the wacky new religions that emerge from time to time. Although the institutional church may not yet have raised up counterfeit "messiahs", it might be argued that in raising up a caste of "priests" to act as go-betweens, supposedly bridging the gap between man and God, even the institutional church has usurped some of the glory of Jesus and applied it falsely to "the church". Many people are confused thereby, and some even deceived.

Jesus goes on (v. 6) to tell us that we will see *wars and rumours of wars* until the end. It is impossible to find any period in history when warfare has been absent. Even when countries are at peace, they are nevertheless wondering when will the next war begin, and are arming themselves for it. This is surely what Jesus meant when He spoke of "rumours" of wars. At the time this book was being written civil war was raging in Syria with the threat of spill-over to neighbouring countries. A new Islamic group had dubbed itself "Islamic State" and was attacking at least three countries in the Middle East and had apparently declared 'holy war' on the Western world. People were asking themselves in the month that these words were being written, will the West "put boots on the ground" to fight-off the Islamic State? That is a rumour of war. When that particular threat declines, there will be others to replace it. There will always be rumours of war.

Yeshua has been totally honest that these things will continue until He returns in glory. Are we to despair of

---

[1] See *Rebel Church – a challenge and an encouragement to the believer* by Peter Sammons. Glory to Glory Publications, 2013. Details in Further Reading section at back of this book.

peace, then? Should we cease to pray and work for peace? Elsewhere Jesus has told us that 'peace-makers' are especially to be blessed. There *will* be opportunities to bring a measure of shalom through divinely-guided human efforts – and that does not just mean an absence of warfare. We think of those who provide food, medical help and shelter to others who are suffering the reality of war. We think of those who bring practical and prayerful help to those suffering persecution. These are rightful and blessed pursuits for a true believer. But the politically-inspired antics of groups such as Christian Peacemaker Teams (whom we met in the Introduction to this book) and the interminable display of biased public demonstrations against this, that and the other, is surely not what Jesus means by being a blessed peacemaker. The idea that somehow we humans are going to create a peaceful world is a false one. It is a false 'promise' that can only lead to dashed hopes. There is a Christian theological construct known as post-millennialism, a subject again well beyond the scope of this book. It teaches that the church will usher in a fresh age when "Christianity" will become the dominant world-view, and usher in an age of unprecedented peace and prosperity. No matter how sincerely this view is held, it runs counter to what Jesus specifically said. *There will be wars and rumours of wars until the very end*. Accordingly post-millenialism must be described as a false doctrine.

We must always remember, again, that *Yeshua* ushers us into His Kingdom – and that is *the place* where His rule is acknowledged and lived out. Perhaps we should say that His Kingdom is *everywhere* where His rule is acknowledged and lived out. In His kingdom there is that measure of peace which is beyond the ability of the 'natural' world to understand, let alone to enjoy. So Jesus tells us that when we are persecuted (and we will be) then we are to rejoice! For then we know with certainty that we belong to Him. We are His people living in accordance with His will – and that inevitably must bring us into conflict with the world's agendas (Matthew 5:9–12).

We are not to go out looking for conflict, but when it arises, we have the joy of knowing that *it is for a purpose* and it proves beyond any doubt that what *Yeshua* has said is true. The apostle Paul emphasised the same point. In his letter to the Philippians, Paul urges the believers to persist in their journey of faith, trying not to worry but instead asking God for what they need. **And God's peace, which is far beyond human understanding, will keep your hearts and minds safe in union with Messiah Jesus** (Philippians 4:7). By keeping our minds fixed upon our true hope, so **"the God who gives us peace"** will continue to guide us (Philippians 4:9). Paul affirmed in a few simple words all that we have been exploring: **God made peace through his son's sacrificial death on the cross and so brought back to himself all things, both on earth and in Heaven** (Colossians 1:20). So it is that God provides the true shalom that we have explored both in the horizontal and vertical axes.

We may face huge difficulties and discomforts in this world – this earthly kingdom.

Colossians is a wonderful and relatively short letter. I will suggest to readers now that they might want to pause and read its four short chapters. ⬭

A Cup and a Stone – and the Fourth World War

Jerusalem – a city with a great past and a great future! As with every aspect of modern and ancient Israel there are innumerable voices speaking about Jerusalem and there is a huge battle for truth. There is even a battle for the derivation of the name Jerusalem! What I give here is a useful distillation of various scholarly currents within this debate. I merely caution readers that understanding Jerusalem, what it is, what it represents and what its future is, is a considerable undertaking where almost inevitably people will approach the subject with certain preconceived notions that may be difficult to shift – even to acknowledge. I invite readers to discard their emotion for a while and try to think calmly and clearly about a very important subject. I would go further. Why not ask the Holy Spirit to counsel you as you approach this subject, to help you to listen carefully for His still, small voice[2] amongst a cacophony of babble about Jerusalem and Israel?

Scholars tell us that the earliest mention of the name occurs in the Egyptian Execration Texts where it may be transliterated *Urusalimum*. As the centuries rolled by it appears to have devolved down to two Semitic elements being *uru* (city) and *salim* (a divine name) and hence may be thought of as city-of-god. Whether "Salim" was also a recognised deity by that name must be problematic and this is where agendas begin to kick-in! The oldest textual evidence, Egyptian, West Semitic and Akkadian, supports only the terms *uru+salim*, and because the Old Testament itself tells us that Jerusalem was not originally a Hebrew city, we can probably agree with a degree of assurance that the oldest name approximated to *city of god*. Linking the names of towns ('cities') with local "gods" was a common practice in the ancient near-East. That Jerusalem was not originally a Hebrew settlement is suggested by Genesis 14:18 where we first encounter the mysterious figure of Melchisedec – and here a whole fresh batch of agendas begin to impact our understanding.[3] Your author will add only this: it seems abundantly clear from any reading of the Bible that the God of Abraham and of Isaac and of Jacob has always had a special plan for the city that we call Jerusalem. That in turn means that Satan, God's adversary, also has designs on the city.

Salim and shalom appear to share the same Semitic root, so again the idea of the *City of Peace* is also a Biblical one.

---

[2] 1 Kings 19:12

[3] Highly recommended book *Melchisedec – A Character Study* by Robert W. Dallmann, published by Christ-Life Inc in USA and widely available via internet in 2015. Dallmann sets out the case with clarity that Melchizedec is in fact a pre-incarnate appearance of Jesus. Having reviewed the biblical reasoning, your author supports this view. This is, however, a completely separate study. See Further Reading details at the end of this book.

Whatever its name, Jerusalem has never been a peaceful city, as so many nations and empires have fought over it incessantly since the beginning of recorded history. Can we discern a spiritual dimension to this incessant warfare?

Among the themes that unify the biblical Book of Isaiah, one of the more notable is that of Jerusalem, or the roughly synonymous Zion, the city of God. The names 'Jerusalem' and 'Zion' appear ninety-seven times in Isaiah. Jerusalem had been a religious centre long before David's forces captured it near the beginning of the tenth century before Messiah (2 Samuel 5:6–8). In the Bible's first mention of that city, we learn that its king, Melchisedec, was also a priest (Genesis 14:18). When David, some eight centuries later, made Jerusalem his capital (see 2 Samuel 5:9), the traditional imagery associated with that ancient priest/king Melchisedec was absorbed into the official imagery of its new king, David. With respect to Israel, David was the successor of Saul. With respect to Jerusalem, however, David was the successor to Melchisedec, whom we find identified as both king and priest in the psalm related to the Davidic throne (Psalm 110; cf. Matthew 22:43–5).

The theme of Jerusalem is treated differently in each of Isaiah's three parts: the prophecies of the Messiah [chapters 1–39], the prophecies of the Servant of the Lord [chapters 40–55], and the prophecies of the Triumphant Warrior [chapters 56–66]. Much of the context of the first part of Isaiah is the reign of Ahaz (735–716), the grandson of Uzziah. It was a period of great, officially-sanctioned religious apostasy, so Isaiah's message to Jerusalem is one of judgement. The book begins with an indictment:

You are doomed, you sinful nation, you corrupt and evil people! Your sins drag you down! You have rejected the Lord, the holy God of Israel, and have turned your backs on him. Why do you keep on rebelling? Do you want to be punished even more? Israel, your head is

already covered with wounds, and your heart and mind are sick [1:4–5].

This theme of impending divine judgment on Jerusalem continues through much of this first part of the prophecy.

In the second part of the book, the prophecies concerning the Servant of the Lord, the historical context is the Babylonian Captivity. The teaching in this part of Isaiah is concerned with Jerusalem's future restoration:

Encourage the people of Jerusalem. Tell them they have suffered long enough and their sins are now forgiven. I have punished them in full for all their sins" [40:2].

And later in that same chapter,

Jerusalem, go up on a high mountain and proclaim the good news! Call out with a loud voice, Zion; announce the good news! Speak out and do not be afraid. Tell the towns of Judah that their God is coming! [40.9].

This theme of restoration continues in the third part of Isaiah, the prophecies of the Triumphant Warrior:

The Lord says to his people, "I will come to Jerusalem to defend you and to save all of you that turn from your sins" [59.20].

What is especially striking about Isaiah's prophecies on Jerusalem is the repetition of images and ideas about the holy city in all parts of the book. For example, in both 35:10 and 51:11 we find,

Those whom you have rescued will reach Jerusalem with gladness, singing and shouting for joy. They will be happy forever, forever free from sorrow and grief.

Again, in 65:25 we read about Jerusalem,

Wolves and lambs will eat together; lions will eat straw, as cattle do, and snakes will no longer be dangerous. On Zion, my sacred hill, there will be nothing harmful or evil.

These images of the holy city had all appeared in the first part of Isaiah [11:6-9].

Readers may again want to pause just now to read Psalm 48 ⌷ which speaks so beautifully of Zion. It is plain that Zion has a special place in God's heart and that all mankind are to marvel at it. The prophecy in Psalm 48 is plainly a *continuing story* – its ideals have not yet been fully realised. For Christians there is a "spiritual" dimension to this which brings both joy and peace. As we look about us in this war -ravaged world, we can rejoice that we are ingrafted to these promises, as we are part of God's family. So, like the ancient Israelites, we marvel at God's love and we rejoice in His judgements (vv. 9–11). We too are encouraged, spiritually, to savour the wonders of Zion (vv. 12–14). One day we will savour the wonders of Zion in a physical sense as well.

In spite of all the wonderful assurances that the Scriptures give about Zion – about Jerusalem – it is a sad fact that the world has its own agendas. Jerusalem is today the most talked about city on the face of this planet – yet it is a tiny one. The United Nations and all the major powers are committed to a *road map to peace* that appears simply to ignore God's holy plans for this, His city of peace. We will not try to be definitive about this matter here, as many others have explored the subject and it probably requires a separate book to examine adequately. The world's *road map to peace* involves setting up non-Jewish ownership of large swathes of *Eretz Israel* and to divide Jerusalem into Israeli (or sometimes 'international') and Muslim control. It involves, in fact, installing a dagger at the heart of Israel and one that would certainly call into question Israel's continued viability as a State. No doubt the international community will offer Israel certain "guarantees" of safety[4] in return for a reduction in control, but their guarantees will be given (if at all) in bad faith.

Some readers may find these astonishing and sweeping statements to make. So much of the Bible points towards a time of unprecedented peace for the people of Israel within their promised land that it is difficult to ignore these prophecies in totality. It is also impossible to apply them solely to "the church" as some have attempted to do. Instead we are forced to accept them at face value – perhaps we should say literally. Without falling into the trap of trying to locate "proof texts" to prove a point, we can nevertheless appeal to the Scriptures on p. 103 as general support for the proposition that God's purposes for Israel and Jerusalem include perpetual peace and a living out of covenant promises (see chart below).

Zechariah is an important prophetic book looking at the restoration of Israel pursuant to its Babylonian captivity, but beyond this, it surely links the Old Testament to the eschatological future – this at least is the understanding of most Bible-believing Christians. It is in Zechariah chapter 12 that we glean a view of an unprecedented future.

This is the word of the LORD concerning Israel. The LORD, who stretches out the heavens, who lays the foundation of the earth, and who forms the spirit of man within him, declares: "I am going to make Jerusalem a cup that sends all the surrounding peoples reeling. Judah will be besieged as well as Jerusalem. On that day, when all the nations of the earth are gathered

---

[4] Many will remember with great sorrow the United Nations' guarantees of 'safe areas' during the Bosnian-Serb conflict of the mid 1990s, when thousands of Serb Muslims were massacred at Srebrenica under the noses of Dutch UN troops who failed to intervene.

GOD'S DEALINGS WITH ISRAEL – THE HEBREW PEOPLE	BIBLE	AUTHOR'S COMMENTS AND QUESTIONS
I will put Israel in her own land, never more to be uprooted	Amos 9: 15	When was this prophecy fulfilled? If it hasn't been fulfilled, when will it be?
All nations will rise up against Israel	Zech 14: 2	Has this prophesy been fulfilled (especially verse 4)? If not when will it be?
God's help to Israel – Israel survives!	Ps 124	But surely this is still true?
God remembers his covenant – and will establish an everlasting covenant	Ezek 16: 60	But surely this is still true?
God's promise of peace to Israel	2 Sam 7: 10 Heb 3: 18 – 4: 1	No longer disturbed ...... has this yet been fulfilled? The Jews were unable to 'enter' because of their unbelief – but will there come a time when they do believe and may therefore enter their rest?
God's plans remain forever	Ps 33:10 - 11	The Lord thwarts the plans of men (and nations) but his plans stand forever. Can we apply this to the Jews?
Future unprecedented peace for Israel?	Isaiah 63: 7	Jer 31:28, 31:36, 32:42, 32:37–41, 33:6-8. When did this happen if not in the future?

**against her, I will make Jerusalem an immovable rock
for all the nations. All who try to move it will injure
themselves. On that day I will strike every horse with
panic and its rider with madness," declares the LORD.
"I will keep a watchful eye over the house of Judah, but
I will blind all the horses of the nations."**

(Zechariah 12:1–4)

In spite of being the City of God, in spite of being in a very
real sense the location of God's peace for all mankind, through
God's covenant and through God's Son, still Jerusalem MUST
represent a huge problem for the nations of the world. They
could, of course, choose to let Israel live out in peace in the
land that God has established for them. They could do so, but
they surely will not. So Jerusalem will be a cup and a stone – to
use the words of Zechariah: **I am going to make Jerusalem
a cup that sends all the surrounding peoples reeling.**

Somehow, it seems that a federation of surrounding peoples
will assault Israel, surely in the vain belief that they can
defeat it, that they can bury it. And yet this doomed plan will
be like a powerful cup of alcohol. Having gulped it down in
sheer ignorance, the guilty countries will reel, like a drunken
man. It will surely bring them crashing down. **When all the
nations of the earth are gathered against her, I will make
Jerusalem an immovable rock for all the nations. All who
try to move it will injure themselves.**

Once again we can only observe that all the nations of Earth
will rise against Israel. This has not yet taken place, but how
close might we be to this? When the nations are not waging
warfare against Israel, they are waging lawfare through the
institutions of the United Nations and international courts,
slowly but surely deligitimizing Israel in the eyes of the
world. In speaking of the *rising of all the nations* of the earth,
we can easily foresee that the United Nations can well be a
proxy for "all the nations" perhaps assembling a coalition of
the willing (a popular modern term) to wipe Israel out – as

104

they assume. They have not, of course, read the end of the story, which the Bible sets out in straightforward terms. They will instead themselves be destroyed. And so it is that the city of peace, the city of God, becomes the locale for man's final rebellion against God.

All this will be preceded by, or accompanied by, unprecedented persecution against Christians – or against those who faithfully follow *Yeshua* as Lord and as Saviour. This world may yet fight a third world war, as superpowers jockey for position, and as angry people everywhere, some of them religiously inspired, stoke the fires of small wars that could easily become huge wars. Jesus has confirmed, there will be wars and rumours of wars until He returns to usher in His age of peace – the millennial rule of the King of kings and Lord of lords. This will happen. I do not know if there will be a third world war, but allowing that there might be, I believe we must also focus on a *fourth world war* – the war of the whole world against one small country the size of Wales – which is simply not allowed to live in peace and security. It is the world's detestation of Israel that will lead ultimately to the end of the world system as we know it. It will lead to God's judgement upon the world. To which the saints must say – halleluiah! God has promised it. God's purposes will not be thwarted. We do not say this with any sense of triumphalism – we say it with a sense of sadness, as many will oppose God's clearly stated purposes. God will not delay forever.

One day the old Jerusalem will be replaced by a new Jerusalem. We read about this at the very end of the Bible. I can only commend Revelation chapter 21 to the diligent reader.

Chapter Seven

OF PRINCES AND KINGS

A peace that passes all understanding

We now "wrap up" all that we have been thinking about: *Yeshua* is identified by His title – Prince of Peace. He was prefigured as such from ancient times. The peace which He brings is a peace which is capable of enjoyment by ALL mankind. The only *human right* that the Bible specifically states is the right to become a child of God – a child with full inheritance rights, moreover, and one who will be with their Father in Heaven throughout eternity. There is a cost to becoming a disciple of *Yeshua*, but that cost is relatively light. The cost to *Yeshua* in making that familial relationship a possibility was infinite. He became sin for us,[1] as all our sins were laid to His account. He pays the cost that we deserved to pay, *and must inevitably pay if we do not avail ourselves of His selfless kindness.* God in His gracious mercy has provided the only remedy for sin that meets His fundamental nature as the God of righteousness. This was (is!) no cheap peace that He provided. It is not peace at any price. No, it is peace that is guaranteed by the blood of Jesus. See Colossians 1:15–23.

I have a friend who once expressed some annoyance that he found me "so certain" of my own salvation. I am unsure what precisely drove that discomfort, unless it was his own fear that he did not enjoy the same certainty. At the time he was dabbling with various philosophies and religions, and was discomforted by the possibility that those of other faiths and

[1] 2 Corinthians 5:21

philosophies did not (could not) enjoy the same certainty of peace with God. I suspect he also "saw" in my certainty what he thought to be self-righteousness – the certainty of a spiritual "big-head" who believes he is better than everyone else! I am sorry if have ever given that impression! My friend's view is probably in fact a common, if seriously awry, prejudice. True Christians are not self-righteous. We cannot possibly be, as we know we could never have saved ourselves. We are "clothed", to use a biblical term, in the righteousness of *Yeshua*. If we are anything, then, far from being self-righteous, we can only be Messiah-righteous – but this does not assuage the world's prejudice, I am afraid! (See Romans 13:14 and Philippians 3:9 which speak into this). We can only say, once again, that the peace which *Yeshua* imparts to his followers is a peace which, in truth, surpasses the ability to comprehend – and yet is real, just the same! (Philippians 4:7).

My friend's challenge, however, caused me to stop and to think. How can I be so certain, and is it wrong to enjoy such certainty? I think it is important to say that I believe that a Christian can lose their faith and accordingly their salvation. This IS NOT the same as having doubts – even serious ones – and struggling. Many Christians will admit to having struggled in this way. Yet most come through their doubts and trials all the more certain – and we praise God for that! And this is NOT the same as saying that sins can knock us off course in our walk with the Lord. They will and they do, from time to time. I say this with no joy and not in a sense of self-satisfaction. As someone once said "being a Christian does not make us sinless, but it does help us to sin less!" The Christian life is both a journey and a battle. Whilst there is no inevitability to failure (perish the thought!) it happens with sufficient frequency to make us realise we need His empowering and His indwelling constantly and we need to reinvigorate our relationship with Him, regularly. Most Christians do this consciously through at least weekly corporate worship, as well as regular (daily) prayer and frequent Bible study. Fellowship with other believers is also essential.

I do not believe, then, in the non-biblical phrase "once saved, always saved" – although this is a massively complex question and one that needs to be worked through with great care. Is it wrong to enjoy such certainty? I will give the biblical reasons for certainty in just a moment, but first we can observe that the many *religions* do not offer this certainty. Rather the opposite. Most DEMAND performance and leave their adherents forever wondering whether their performance has been sufficient to "do the trick" with their deity. We are told, for example, that the only way a Muslim can be certain of going to paradise is if they die actively engaged in military jihad, something that may explain the fervour with which some Muslim males, in particular, are attracted to this mechanism. How do we contrast the Christian's certainty with the teachings of the various religions?

In fact we do not need to do so. There is no real comparability between the many religions and true biblical Christianity. As we say in the UK, *you need to compare apples with apples*, so there is little point in making what must ultimately be spurious comparisons.[2] The world's faith systems are fundamentally incompatible. So how is it then that Christianity can offer such assurance to disciples of *Yeshua*? There seem to be three ways of addressing this. And at this point I will depart from my earlier promise not to provide "proof texts" that are aimed to settle a question. The whole book up to this point has set out carefully the promise of peace through the Prince of Peace. By this stage readers should at the very least have acquired a measure of understanding of what this shalom is, and how it may be obtained. So the three key points I will make below will only serve to reinforce what has been explored before. The three ways in which we can

---

[2] Once again, readers who feel a definite need to explore this subject in a little more detail might want to access the author's book *The Empty Promise of Godism*. See further reading section at the back of this book.

THE PRINCE OF PEACE

address the questions of assurance are these:

Jesus said it
Luke 18:17 – accept like a child ....
John 4:14 – whoever drinks ... will never thirst ....
John 3:1–21 – especially v. 15 –what rebirth means....
John 17:3 – this is eternal life ....
(The Lord will not forsake His disciples)
John 6:37–39   John 10:28   Matthew 28:20

The Bible affirms it
Ephesians 1:4–7 – we have redemption through the blood...
1 John 2:2 – the atoning sacrifice ....
1 John 5:11–13 – life is in His Son ....
1 Peter 3:18 – Christ died, once for ALL ....
Romans 3:21–25 – righteousness through faith ....
Romans 4:25–Jesus was raised for this ....
Romans 8:38–39 – He will never leave you ....
Romans 10:9 – if you confess you will be saved ....

The whole of history points towards it
Ephesians 1:9 – when the times had reached their
fulfilment.
John 1:1 and 12 – in the beginning ... God gave them the
right to become children of God ....
Exodus 14 – crossing the Red Sea – a "type" of the
crossing over from death to life.
(Messianic prophecies, e.g.)
Isaiah 52 and 53 – the Suffering Servant ....
Jeremiah 31:31-34 – the New Covenant foretold .....
Isaiah 42:6 – the covenant extends to all nations ....
Exodus 12 – The Passover and the marking of doors with
blood (a "type" of the work of Yeshua on the cross at
Passover in Jerusalem).

The answer to my friend, then, has to be in the witness of the entire Bible on this subject. God has a plan – the Bible has a meta-narrative. It is the story of salvation. And as someone once said "all history is His-Story". We can be certain of God's righteousness as well as His great love. What is the key measure of God's love? It is in this: Romans 5:8 (look it up!) So assurance must inevitably bring us true shalom – true peace. It is not a big-headed shalom because we know we could not have achieved it ourselves. It is a confident shalom in the finished work of *Yeshua ha Massiach* (Jesus the Messiah) on the cross of crucifixion. It is a peace for me. And it is a peace for you! Remember our formula in the previous chapter: A + B + C = L/P.

We sense then that the case is now made. The *Prince of Peace* (or Prince Shalom) does indeed give His peace and it is a joy to live in His power and in His service, albeit sometimes that is a fitful service on our part.

Becoming a disciple of Jesus leads to a completely new identity in Christ. There seem to be three key categories of identity in Christianity as suggested by the following short study, which readers may want to follow through as a separate exercise. These categories of identity are *acceptance* by God, *security* in God and *significance* in God. A true believer then can confidently claim:

I am accepted
I am God's child – John 1:12
I am Christ's friend – John 15:15
I have been justified – Romans 5:1
I am united with the Lord, and one in spirit with Him –
1 Corinthians 6:17
I have been bought with a price and belong to God –
1 Corinthians 6:19–20
I am a saint – Ephesians 1:1
I have been adopted as God's child – Ephesians 1:5
I have direct access to God through the Holy Spirit –
Ephesians 2:18

I have been redeemed and forgiven of all my sins –
Colossians 1:14
I am complete in Christ – Colossians 2:10

I am secure
I am free from condemnation – Romans 8:1–2
I am assured that all things work together for the good of
those who love God.... – Romans 8:28a
I am free from any condemning charges against me –
Romans 8:31
I cannot be separated from the love of God – Romans 8:35
I have been established, anointed and sealed by God –
2 Corinthians 1:21–22
I am hidden with Christ in God – Colossians 3:3
I have not been given a spirit of fear but of power, love and
self control – 2 Timothy 1:7
I can find grace and mercy in time of need – Hebrews 4:16
I am born of God, and the evil one cannot harm me –
1 John 5:18

I am significant
I am the salt and light of the earth – Matthew 5:13–14
I am a branch of the true vine if I remain in Jesus – John
15:1ff.
I have been chosen and appointed to bear fruit – John
15:16
I am meant to be a personal witness of Christ – Acts 1:8
I am God's co-worker – 1 Corinthians 3:9 and
2 Corinthians 6:1
I am seated with Christian the heavenly realms – Ephesians
2:6
I am God's workmanship – Ephesians 2:10
I may approach God with freedom and confidence –
Ephesians 3:12
I can do all things through Christ Who strengthens me –
Philippians 4:13

Readers will see that these are pretty amazing claims to make. True biblical Christianity is not so much a religion as a relationship – the relationship of a child to their loving and holy Father through Jesus Christ, the Father's Son.

Why not the King of Peace?

What does it mean to speak of Jesus as the "Christ"? This word is one of the most important basic words in a Christian's vocabulary. Strangely, many Christians have great difficulty in explaining what it means. Some people think it is the Lord's surname! However it is a word with considerable implications. The word "Christ" comes from *christos*, a Greek word meaning "anointed". It is the equivalent of the word *mashiach* or Messiah in Hebrew. So to be the Christ, or Messiah, is to be "the anointed one of God". Indeed it is correctly said that in English, Christians could just as easily be called "Messiahns"!

To be anointed, literally, is to have sacred oil poured upon one's head, because God has chosen that person for a special role. Priests and kings were anointed, and sometimes prophets. Kings were anointed during their coronation rather than receiving a crown. Even though prophets and priests were anointed, the phrase "anointed one" or "the Lord's anointed" was most often used to refer to a king. For instance, David used it many times to refer to King Saul, even when Saul was trying to murder him and David was on the verge of killing Saul to defend himself:

"The Lord forbid that I should do such a thing to my master, the Lord's anointed, or lift my hand against him; for he is the anointed of the Lord" (1 Samuel 24:6, NIV).

The overriding biblical imagery involved in the word "Messiah" is that of a king chosen by God. Often in the Old

Testament, God would tell a prophet to go and anoint someone
and proclaim him king. The act of anointing with sacred
oil emphasised that it was *God himself* who had ordained a
person and given him authority to act as his representative.
Throughout the Old Testament (*The Promise* that we referred
to in Chapter 1), we see hints that God will one day send a
great king to Israel who would eventually rule the world. In
Genesis, when Jacob blesses each of his sons and foretells
his own future, he says of Judah:

**The sceptre will not depart from Judah, nor the ruler's
staff from between his feet, until he comes to whom it
belongs and the obedience of the nations is his**.

(Genesis 49:10, NIV)

This is the first hint that they were to expect a great king to
arise out of Israel who would be king over the whole earth.
The clearest prophecy about the future messianic king comes
from King David's time. David earnestly desired to build a
temple, a "house" for God, but God responded that David's
son Solomon would be the one to build his temple. But then
God went on to promise He would build a "house" for David,
meaning that God would establish his family line after him.
He further promised that from David's family would come a
king whose kingdom will have no end:

**"When your days are over and you go to be with your
fathers, I will raise up your offspring to succeed you,
one of your own sons, and I will establish his kingdom.
He is the one who will build a house for me, and I will
establish his throne forever. I will be his father, and he
will be my son. I will never take my love away from him,
as I took it away from your predecessor. I will set him
over my house and my kingdom forever; his throne will
be established forever"** (1 Chronicles 17:11–14, NIV).

This prophecy is understood by most Christian commentators as having a double fulfilment. It is first fulfilled in Solomon, who built the Temple, but who then did what God forbade — amassed a great fortune and married foreign wives. His kingdom disintegrated a few years after his death. But this prophecy looks forward to a "Son of David" who would come, and who would have a kingdom without end. This, in fact, is the basis of all the messianic prophecies that speak of the "Son of David" and the coming messianic king.

The Gospels use cultural images of kingship to proclaim *Yeshua* as the Messiah, God's anointed King who has come. When a king arose with great power, other kingdoms would send emissaries with lavish gifts to establish a friendly relationship with the future leader. This surely was what happened in Matthew 2, when magi came to bring gifts to *Yeshua*, the newborn king whose star they had seen in the East. (This was a fulfilment of Numbers 24:17, Isaiah 60, and Psalm 72. The latter two passages both describe the coming of a great king and state that representatives from nations everywhere will come to give Him tribute). We see a further image of *Yeshua* as King when He rode the donkey into Jerusalem. This was often part of the announcement of a new king, as it was for Solomon in 1 Kings 1:38–39. It is the fulfilment of Zechariah 9:9, the triumphal entry of the messianic king.

Rejoice greatly, O Daughter of Zion! Shout, Daughter of Jerusalem! See, your king comes to you, righteous and having salvation, gentle and riding on a donkey, on a colt, the foal of a donkey (Zech 9:9, NIV).

Yeshua explained that His kingdom was not of this world (John 18:37). Rather, *Yeshua* was teaching about the kingdom of God, the major locus of His preaching. The kingdom of God is comprised of those who submit their lives to *Yeshua* as Lord and as Saviour. As the King that God has sent, the kingdom of God is *Yeshua*'s kingdom. He speaks about how it is expanding like yeast or mustard seed. The good news spreads that He has arrived and people accept Him as King. When He returns in glory, every knee on earth will bow to honour him as King (Philippians 2:9).

The fact that *Yeshua*'s disciples and others who believed in Him referred to him as "Lord" suggests that they were giving him great honour, with their understanding that He was the Messiah-King. To call Jesus "Lord" was to use a term for addressing royalty, like saying "Your Majesty" or "Your Highness". It was also a common term for addressing God himself, and hints, therefore, of worshiping *Yeshua* as God. To use the word "Lord" implies an attitude of obedient submission. *Yeshua* seems to have expected that those who call Him "Lord" would obey him. To His listeners He asked, **"Why do you call me 'Lord, Lord,' and do not do what I say**?" (Luke 6:46, NIV). To call Him "Lord" or to call Him Jesus Messiah or "Christ" is to say that He is the King that God has sent Who has the right to reign over us.

This has natural follow-on implications about how we define ourselves as Christian believers. Often we think in terms of doctrines and beliefs, but the very word Messiah (or "Christ") means far more than simply assenting to a creed. If "Christ" means King, a Christian is one who considers Jesus to be his Lord and King, and submits to His reign. The apostle Paul also proclaimed that salvation comes through faith in the atoning work of *Yeshua*, as well as a commitment to honour Jesus as our personal Lord and King:

If you confess with your mouth Jesus as Lord, and believe in your heart that God raised him from the dead, you will be saved (Romans 10:9, NIV).

Why then was the coming Messiah prophesied as the Prince of Peace? Why not the King of Peace? We should perhaps not read too much into this distinction, but it surely has to do with the fact that in *Yeshua*'s (Jesus') first incarnation He was not yet recognised by His own people (the Hebrews) nor by the wider world. He had authority, as any prince would, but not at that stage the power that attends the authority. So He is "King" at present only to those who acknowledge Him as such, and into their lives He pours out His peace – His wonderful shalom, that the world at large simply cannot understand. He is King, of His Kingdom, but as we have seen this kingdom is not presently "of" this world. One day when He returns in His second incarnation, His rule will be absolute and complete. Then the Lord will be known by a number of titles, but one of these will undoubtedly be "The King of Peace". What better way to end this book than with a Bible verse. Let us make it our prayer four ourselves and those we love:

May the God who gives us peace make you holy in every way and keep your whole being --spirit, soul, and body – free from every fault at the coming of our Lord Jesus Christ. He who calls you will do it, because he is faithful (1 Thessalonians 5:23–24, NIV).

APPENDIX 1

Select list – OT Prophecies about the Messiah and their NT fulfilment

Prophecies about Jesus	Old Testament Scripture	New Testament Fulfilment
1. Messiah would be born of a woman.	Genesis 3:15	Matthew 1:20 Galatians 4:4
2. Messiah would be born in Bethlehem.	Micah 5:2	Matthew 2:1 Luke 2:4-6
3. Messiah would be born of a virgin.	Isaiah 7:14	Matthew 1:22-23 Luke 1:26-31
4. Messiah would come from the line of Abraham.	Genesis 12:3 Genesis 22:18	Matthew 1:1 Romans 9:5
5. Messiah would be a descendant of Isaac.	Genesis 17:19 Genesis 21:12	Luke 3:34
6. Messiah would be a descendant of Jacob.	Numbers 24:17	Matthew 1:2
7. Messiah would come from the tribe of Judah.	Genesis 49:10	Luke 3:33 Hebrews 7:14
8. Messiah would be heir to King David's throne.	2 Samuel 7:12-13 Isaiah 9:7	Luke 1:32-33 Romans 1:3
9. Messiah's throne will be anointed and eternal.	Psalm 45:6-7 Daniel 2:44	Luke 1:33 Hebrews 1:8-12
10. Messiah would be called Immanuel.	Isaiah 7:14	Matthew 1:23
11. Messiah would spend a season in Egypt.	Hosea 11:1	Matthew 2:14-15
12. A massacre of children would happen at Messiah's birthplace.	Jeremiah 31:15	Matthew 2:6-18
13. A messenger would prepare the way for Messiah	Isaiah 40:3-5	Luke 3:3-6
14. Messiah would be rejected by his own people.	Psalm 69:8 Isaiah 53:3	John 1:11 John 7:5
15. Messiah would be a prophet.	Deuteronomy 18:15	Acts 3:20-22

16. Messiah would be preceded by Elijah.	Malachi 4:5-6	Matthew 11:13-14
17. Messiah would be declared the Son of God.	Psalm 2:7	Matthew 3:16-17
18. Messiah would be called a Nazarene.	Isaiah 11:1	Matthew 2:23
19. Messiah would bring light to Galilee.	Isaiah 9:1-2	Matthew 4:13-16
20. Messiah would speak in parables.	Psalm 78:2-4 Isaiah 6:9-10	Matthew 13:10-15, 34-35
21. Messiah would be sent to heal the brokenhearted.	Isaiah 61:1-2	Luke 4:18-19
22. Messiah would be a priest after the order of Melchizedek.	Psalm 110:4	Hebrews 5:5-6
23. Messiah would be called King.	Psalm 2:6 Zechariah 9:9	Matthew 27:37 Mark 11:7-11
24. Messiah would be praised by little children.	Psalm 8:2	Matthew 21:16
25. Messiah would be betrayed.	Psalm 41:9 Zechariah 11:12-13	Luke 22:47-48 Matthew 26:14-16
26. Messiah's price money would be used to buy a potter's field.	Zechariah 11:12-13	Matthew 27:9-10
27. Messiah would be falsely accused.	Psalm 35:11	Mark 14:57-58
28. Messiah would be silent before his accusers.	Isaiah 53:7	Mark 15:4-5
29. Messiah would be spat upon and struck.	Isaiah 50:6	Matthew 26:67
30. Messiah would be hated without cause.	Psalm 35:19 Psalm 69:4	John 15:24-25

31. Messiah would be crucified with criminals.	Isaiah 53:12	Matthew 27:38 Mark 15:27-28
32. Messiah would be given vinegar to drink.	Psalm 69:21	Matthew 27:34 John 19:28-30
33. Messiah's hands and feet would be pierced.	Psalm 22:16 Zechariah 12:10	John 20:25-27
34. Messiah would be mocked and ridiculed.	Psalm 22:7-8	Luke 23:35
35. Soldiers would gamble for Messiah's garments.	Psalm 22:18	Luke 23:34 Matthew 27:35-36
36. Messiah's bones would not be broken.	Exodus 12:46 Psalm 34:20	John 19:33-36
37. Messiah would be forsaken by God.	Psalm 22:1	Matthew 27:46
38. Messiah would pray for his enemies.	Psalm 109:4	Luke 23:34
39. Soldiers would pierce Messiah's side.	Zechariah 12:10	John 19:34
40. Messiah would be buried with the rich.	Isaiah 53:9	Matthew 27:57-60
41. Messiah would resurrect from the dead.	Psalm 16:10 Psalm 49:15	Matthew 27:57-60 Matthew 28:2-7 Acts 2:22-32
42. Messiah would ascend to heaven.	Psalm 24:7-10	Mark 16:19 Luke 24:51
43. Messiah would be seated at God's right hand.	Psalm 68:18 Psalm 110:1	Mark 16:19 Matthew 22:44
44. Messiah would be a sacrifice for sin.	Isaiah 53:5-12	Romans 5:6-8

APPENDIX 2

THE GOD WHO MAKES AND KEEPS COVENANTS

Reproduced from *Rebel Church* (Glory to Glory Publications)

God is a promise-keeping God. He makes His covenants and we must respond to those covenants, either in faith or rejection.

Which covenants are still in force? The table on the next two pages suggests it is only the Moses covenant that has been replaced – and that it has been replaced by the Messianic covenant, which ushers in a new age.

Each covenant has been given a number for ease of reference. Each row in the table shows with whom the covenant was established, and its conditionality.

Note to Appendix 2

Does this matter? Is this just ancient history or dry theology? Many Christians hold that these truths speak into our situation today; in particular into the world in which we currently live, the growth of the Messianic Jewish movement and the restoration of the Jewish people to their biblical home land. Are these accidents of history, or is God working out his covenantal promises as He said He would? Finally, these texts help us to understand which covenants are timeless and therefore still apply. Crucially they suggest that it is the Moses covenant that has been 'replaced', by being extended and enlarged to cover all mankind. Today God appoints a royal priesthood of all those who are true disciples of Jesus.

	Made with	Key text	Commentary
0	Adam	Gen 2:16	We are free to live in peace and to enjoy all that God gives. We are not, however, free to sin without consequence. Whilst this is not truly a covenant, it is included in this list to give perspective to the other five covenants.
1	Noah	Gen 9:16	God in fact made an extended covenant with Noah, in terms of protecting Noah and his family. Gen 6:18; Gen 8:21b; Gen 9:3 (reminiscent of Gen 1:29); Gen 9:11 through 17.
2	Abraham	Gen 12:2-3	Repeated and emphasised: Gen 12:7; Gen 15:5-7; Gen 22:16-18; Ex 3:8, Ex 3:17; Ex 6:6-8
3	Moses	Ex 19:5-6	The Hebrews become a nation of priests: this is a blessing to the whole world. Ex 20 (all) and Ex 34:10ff set out the conditions applicable.
4	David	2 Sam 7:13-16	God promises to establish a house for Himself forever (2 Sam 7:13). This is a direct Messianic promise, as God works out His purpose to bless all Mankind. See 1 Sam 16:13. Also 2 Sam 7 (all) and 2 Sam 23:5.
5	Messianic		Having established His covenant with Israel through Abraham and promised a House through David, the covenantal promises now become more explicit, as God points towards what the Messianic office entails, how the Messianic line would bring life from death, and Who that Messiah would be - principally in terms of the suffering servant. God reveals these truths through three major prophets:
5A	Jeremiah (what)	Jer 24:7; Jer 31:31-40	The promise of a new covenant becomes explicit. Jeremiah chapter 33 (all) links the promise of restoration with the Land and through the line of David. It foretells both the Messiah and a future age of peace and righteousness yet to be seen.
5B	Ezekiel (how)	Ezek 37 (all)	Ezekiel 37 shows how God will bring life from death. The restoration of the Jewish Nation, and through them, the provision of the Messiah of the whole world.
5C	Isaiah (who)	Is 52:13 -53:12	The suffering servant becomes explicit: Is 8:14; 9:1-7; 11:1-5; 32:1-4; 50:2-8; and Is 52:13-53:12; and Is 54 through to 56:8

	Made with	Applies to	Conditionality
0	Adam	Through Adam, applies to all mankind	The conditionality is only spelled out in God's gracious refusal to allow mankind to eat from the tree of life (Gen 3:22)
1	Noah	All mankind	Unconditional
2	Abraham	Through the Hebrews, applies to all mankind	Unconditional
3	Moses	The Hebrews	Conditional on obedience
4	David	David	Unconditional
5	Messianic		
5A	Jeremiah (what)	Through the Hebrews, applies to all mankind	Conditional on obedience
5B	Ezekiel (how)	Through the Hebrews, applies to all mankind	Conditional on obedience
5C	Isaiah (who)	Through the Hebrews, applies to all mankind	Conditional on obedience

APPENDIX 3

LOVE

Reproduced from *The Bible Student* (Glory to Glory Publications)

Background: the different kinds of 'love'

'Love' is a term that is often encountered in Christian theology and ethics. However, we must note at the outset that as a word in the English language it is very ambiguous, covering disparate meanings. It is used to translate a number of different words from the Greek New Testament, each of which has a different meaning in the original language there. So there is scope for a great deal of confusion and misunderstanding.

In biblical usage there is a strongly moral sense to this word – something often forgotten by those who sentimentalise biblical references to the love of God (of which there are fewer than many Christians imagine). Of the Greek words that are now loosely translated as 'love', *eros* (sexual attraction/love) does not appear in the New Testament. The Greek *phileo*, signifying natural affection (with more feeling than reason) occurs twenty-five times, with *philadelphia* (brotherly love) five times, and *philia* (friendship) occurring in James 4:4, but also, very importantly (from the same *phileo* root) in the last two of Jesus' three questions addressed to Peter in John 21. By far the most frequent Greek biblical word translated into English as 'love' is *agape*, generally taken to signify a moral good rather than attraction. Agape includes doing good to the undeserving and the unattractive person. It can involve meeting a need. The difference between *agape* and *phileo* may be difficult to comprehend in all passages. (See Note 1.)

True love does not come naturally to fallen man (e.g. the love that causes a man to pray for his enemies; Matthew 5:44). Love in its highest 'agape' form has been revealed in the Lord Jesus Christ.

John writes that 'God is [agape] love' (1 John 4:8) but he is not thereby saying that love is all that God is. Rather, this

127

statement is a message addressed to believers (as, of course, all the epistles are); the context is relational – the relationship between the believer and God – and has to do with believing, and confessing Jesus, and abiding in him. It is made clear that the love of which God is the perfect source is to be reflected in the lives of his people. (1 John 4:8–21.)

The way each of the persons of the Holy Trinity relates to the other two persons is love, so love is in the godhead. We take from this great truth that it was not loneliness that prompted God to create human beings in his image, rather it was his will to share his perfect love with others. This helps us to define the nature of love in its purest form. It is 'my best for another's best'. Agape love which should exist amongst believers towards each other, instead of being self-centred, is focused on the welfare of another person. This kind of loving is truly godly for it reflects something of the very nature of God himself. It also follows that failure to love like this is to fall short of the glory of God: it is sin (Romans 3:23). At the Fall, Adam and Eve put themselves at the centre instead of God and became tainted with sin (disobedience to God). The devil tempted them to sin; that sinfulness has been passed on to all of us (Romans 3:10–18). Thus there was a gulf between man and God to deal with, and only God could provide what we need. When Jesus Christ came into the world and gave his life as the sacrifice for our sin, that was agape love. Jesus, true God and true man, opened up the only way for man to have the righteousness without which it is impossible to relate to a perfectly holy God.

God shows his love for us in that: 'While we were still sinners, Christ died for us' (see Romans 5:8). Jesus always put his Father first, and could say: "Whoever has seen me has seen the Father" (see John 14:8–11). Perfect love shows the character of Christ (see Ephesians 3:19). Love includes: praying for enemies, as we have seen, and putting the Lord first (see Matthew 10:37). It is patient, kind, and not envious, boastful, arrogant, rude, self-seeking, irritable, resentful (bearing grudges), and it is not glad when there is wrongdoing. Love is long-suffering, eager to believe the best, hopes in all circumstances, endures no matter what happens, and never comes to an end. (See 1 Corinthians 13:4–8). Love banishes fear (1 John 4:18), and does no wrong to a neighbour (Romans 13:10). Love delights in serving (Galatians 5:13). It is not worldly (see 1 John 2:15–17).

We cannot do all this in our *own* strength, for in our natural, fallen state we all tend to put ourselves and our interests before the good of others. Our own efforts are inadequate. Spiritual giftedness is no substitute for it (1 Corinthians 12:31–13:3); good works are no substitute for it (1 Corinthians 13:3; Titus 3:5); even a martyr's death is no substitute for it (1 Corinthians 13:3).

Godly love is of God and must be God's own doing in us through the Holy Spirit (Galatians 5:22–23). All need to be 'born again' of water and Spirit. We can then be aware of Christ in [us], 'the hope of glory' (see Colossians 1:27). The way of life and love is made available to sinners who repent and believe in the Lord Jesus Christ, who are baptised in Holy Spirit and go on being filled with the Holy Spirit. It is the calling of those who belong to Christ to live their lives in step with the Holy Spirit. As fruit grows unconsciously upon the branches of a tree, so agape love will grow and appear unconsciously in the personality of believers, as the Spirit works in their lives and they co-operate in that life. Fruit could not survive if it were only tied onto branches! In the same way, this genuinely Christlike life of true love springs from regeneration – though, after regeneration, much sanctification and reforming of thinking has still to occur as we let our minds be renewed by God's word!

John 3:6–21; 13:35; 15:1–5; Romans 5:5; 8:35–39; Ephesians 2:4–6, 5:2; Philippians 2:12–13; 2 Timothy 1:13; 2 Peter 1:3–11; 3:18; 1 John 4:7–8, 16.

Love in the fellowship: a truly New Testament perspective
We have said a good deal about the life of agape love that
must mark the life of believers – and an extremely important
point to note is that this is *corporate* as well as personal. Many
commands of Jesus in the Gospels, as well as the teachings of
the apostles in their letters, are *addressed to believers about
relating to each other*. These instructions are to shape the life
of churches (fellowships of Christians) teaching them about
how brothers and sisters in Christ are to behave with one
another. This is a salutary message, and often a dimension
of New Testament teaching rather unfamiliar to believers
today, who may be less aware of the corporate aspect of the
fellowship of disciples in an individualistic age and culture.
The New Testament teaching about love applies to every
disciple of Jesus today personally, and to every group of
Christians who meet together too.

**Our agape love toward God: an essential that is easy to
miss!**
We have considered *God's agape love* expressed in the single
act in which he once gave his only-begotten Son as the perfect
sacrifice for our sin so that we might not perish but instead
have eternal life. We have also considered the agape love that
believers in the fellowship are to have for each other. But there
is another vital kind of agape love that disciples are to have:
the agape love of the believer toward Jesus Christ. Again,
this is a dimension which is often missed, yet it is essential in
the Christian Way. What exactly is *this* kind of agape love? It
is obviously somewhat different from God's love toward us,
for as we have seen he has provided for our greatest need in
the person of his Son Jesus Christ. God himself has no 'need'
that we could meet as he is perfect and he owns everything
anyway! There is a popular misconception about what our
love toward God is (or should be) like. There is a 'sentimental'
view of the matter which says it is like being 'in love' with
Jesus. However, that way of putting it is a usage in English

which does not express the key that Jesus provided. Happily, Jesus did speak of the kind of love that every disciple is to have *toward God* and it is extremely simple – straightforward enough for even the most uneducated believer to understand and live out. Jesus said: "If you keep my commandments, you will abide in my [agape] love, just as I have kept my Father's commandments and abide in his love" (John 14:10); and, "If you love [agape] me, keep my commandments" (John 14:15). The message is clear: obedience is central. Moreover, it is a message directed to those who are already believers, so that they will continue, persevere, *abide* in (agape) love. They are not to fall into disobedience to God; they are not to wander away into a position of unbelief or to adopt immoral ways of behaving.

It is recommended that the Bible student should study chapters 14–17 of John's Gospel with these three questions in mind: What did Jesus say concerning the love God has towards the disciples, and about the love we are to have toward himself (Jesus), and about the love believers are to have toward each other? Such study will reveal that the love of God is very far from being 'unconditional', a word that does not appear in scripture but which is often heard nowadays! Jesus often says "If...." Note carefully the points at which he does so, in order to understand and minister the word of truth faithfully to others.

So what of John 3:16, a verse considered by many to be the most important in the whole Bible, which includes the words '. . . for God so loved the world . . .' ? Once again, a problem arises in translation. The word often rendered 'so' means 'thus' and refers back to something else – the event referred to in John 3:14 in fact! From v. 14 we learn that God gave his Son *thus – in the same way* as Moses lifted up the snake in the desert. The snake on the pole in that context was used by God to provide the way sinners could avoid the death sentence for the sin of grumbling, for which they were being punished in the desert. That was why they were being killed by the snakes, as a punishment for their sin. 'Thus' or 'so' indicates how Jesus being lifted up (on the cross) is, in the same way, the only means by which humans may have their sins forgiven and so be freed from the sentence of death that sin deserves.

People tend to think that John 3:16 means God *loves* (in a continuous sense) the world *so* much that he gave his Son. But it really means that God acted once in the sacrifice of Jesus (in agape love), and the past aorist Greek tense is used, signifying a one-time act of love (meeting a need in unworthy sinners whose sins deserve death). The one sacrifice was sufficient to meet anyone's need for forgiveness if they would go on believing in Jesus. It is a verse which, when properly understood, encourages the believer to go on believing and so to go on having eternal life. (See Note 2.)

It is also a verse that, if properly understood, may help the unsaved sinner to see that Jesus' once for all sacrifice can be their means of salvation, too.

Notes

[1] For a full treatment of this vital subject, refer to a good Bible encyclopedia. The Baker Encyclopedia of the Bible is highly recommended. Some of the comments above are indebted to that publication, but have been adapted.

[2] See David Pawson, *Is John 3:16 the Gospel?* (Anchor Recordings).

APPENDIX 4

PREPARING THE GROUND –
HOW TO READ A BIBLICAL TEXT
Reproduced from *Prepare the Way!* by Alex Jacob
(Glory to Glory Publications)

As a Christian, I understand that the Bible is the supreme authority for what we as Christians believe and how we try to live. I understand that this authority flows from the sovereignty of God. God is sovereign not just in His engagement with humanity, but also in His revelation of Himself to humanity. The Bible is a factor and a component part in the redeeming work of God, as the Bible accurately and fully communicates God's ways and His redeeming acts. The Bible also teaches how humanity should respond in the light of God's redeeming acts. Therefore, how we read, teach, preach and apply the message of the Bible is of very great importance.

"I have sought Your face with all my heart" (Psalm 119:58)
In terms of understanding any biblical text in a spiritually reflective and faithful way, I believe that there are certain steps which need to be taken by the reader/hearer. My starting point is based on the belief that the meaning of any biblical text is not hidden away in some obscure secret zone, which results in a text only being understandable by (or revealed to) a select few, who have special interpretive skills or who are part of an elect group. Such a view would have been promoted by certain Gnostic sects and by practitioners of parts of the Kabbalistic tradition today, but rather, I believe that God in His revelation through Scripture desires to make the Scriptures clear (the perspicacity of Scripture) and the truths they contain consistent to any and all sincere readers/hearers of the text through the illumination of the Holy Spirit.

Equally God does not make the truths of His Word known to the casual observer, or the proud self-centred student, but

God does make His Word known to the humble sincere seeker. Therefore, the first step in gaining a true understanding of any biblical text is to examine our life and our motivation for gaining understanding and to try and develop a sincere heartfelt desire to gain godly understanding.

"May my cry come before You O Lord; give me understanding according to Your word" (Psalm 119:169)
The second step which flows from the first, is to set time and space aside to read the text carefully and prayerfully. As we mull the text over in our minds, we ask for God's help in engaging with and understanding the text. A prayer along the lines of the following can be helpful: *"Lord help me to understand Your word, set me free from a false worldview or rash insights but rather renew my mind and deepen my capacity to receive Your truth by the gentle work of Your Holy Spirit."*

"Do your best to present yourself to God as one approved, a workman who does not need to be ashamed and who correctly handles the word of truth" (2 Timothy 2:15).
The third step is to invest time in studying the text. A good study of a text begins with assessing the grammatical, historical and textual context of a text. A text should be interpreted initially by its most plain meaning. Words should be interpreted consistently in the same context. A word can have a number of meanings, but only one true meaning in each case in terms of the author's intent. Also the first time a word or idea is introduced it will bring with it certain information which should help to guide in regards to the future understanding of other usage (principle of first use) of the word. Equally, a text may have many useful applications, but I think it can only have one central meaning based on the author's intent. In this initial step of study one should also take into account literary genres, symbolism (figurative and non-figurative symbolism) and figures of speech. Also

in recognising prophetic texts, one must see that a prophecy can have an immediate historical context, a later historical context, or even a yet to be fulfilled future context. Also prophecies may be conditional or unconditional, specific or general in their application.

From this good beginning within the area of study, it is important to go on to explore historical questions based upon the text. For example, who is the author, when was it written, to whom was it written and for what purpose? In attempting to answer these questions we need to draw on the insights of various commentators, theologians and scholars. As we weigh up their insights it seems to me that one can place such insights and ideas on a scale which ranges from the impossible, to the possible, on to the probable and ending with the definite. Also we begin to see how a particular idea or theme fits in with other biblical texts (the principle of correlation) written by the same author and then on to texts from other sources. In this way, I believe one sees how Scripture interprets, clarifies and affirms Scripture.

"When you come together, everyone has a hymn or a word of instruction, a revelation, a tongue or an interpretation. All of these must be done for the strengthening of the church" (1 Corinthians 14:26).

The fourth step is to share and discuss the fruits of our study with others. I believe group Bible studies are very important as we learn from and challenge each other's interpretation and understanding. It is often only in as group context that we discover the complexity of a text, or perhaps the different layers of understanding within a text. I think it is especially helpful when such study groups are made up of Christians who have different backgrounds, or come from different church traditions and who also have a range of life experiences. We learn as we listen and engage with each other. We make space to discern the authenticity of the Holy Spirit's work in and through each other. We also recognise and value those amongst us who have particular teaching gifts within the church and who reflect Christ-like pastoral wisdom.

"Do not merely listen to the word, and so deceive yourselves. Do what it says" (James 1:22).

The fifth step is to apply the text to our lives. Study in not meant to be an end in itself, but rather we study in order to revere God, to worship and to serve obediently and effectively. Sometimes the application of a text is very straightforward. It may not be easy to apply, but nevertheless it is clear. At other times with other texts it is not clear how we apply such understanding, but we store away our insight. Maybe in the future the application of that insight may become clear or the understanding from that text may help in interpreting and applying other texts.

"The Spirit searches all things, even the deep things of God" (1 Corinthians 2:10).

The sixth and final step is to reflect upon how we (and others) have applied a textual understanding. Maybe with experience and the promptings of the Spirit, we feel the text has been misunderstood in some way or perhaps misused or even abused. Maybe a new historical, cultural or personal context means that we seek to apply the text in a different way? As we reflect upon these six steps, we also know that we never come to the end of learning from and engaging with a biblical text.

The full truth of God can never be fully pinned down. No method of biblical study can fully capture the grandeur of the Lord and His ways. The Lord always has more light to give to us, and to bring to His revealed Word. Therefore, the six steps of interpretation do not take us on a linear journey to a single goal of personal insight, but rather along a deepening circle of lifelong study and committed discipleship. Discipleship enriched by being part of a Christian community and inspired and empowered by the powerful prompting and gentle calling of the Holy Spirit.

Further Reading

Bates, Peter
You Can Believe This! – Why biblical Christianity Makes Sense
(Diggory Press Ltd, 2007) ISBN 978-1-84685-784-3

Crombie, Kelvin
In Covenant with Jesus
(Mundaring Australia, 2012)
ISBN 978-0-9873630-0-8 Available through CMJ-UK in Europe.

Dallmann, Robert W.
Melchisedec – A Character Study
(ChristLife Inc, Niagara Falls USA, 2013)

Jacob, Alex
The Case for Enlargement Theology (2nd edition)
(Glory to Glory Publications, 2011) ISBN 978-0-9567831-1-0
*Prepare the Way! – a biblical exploration of four key advent themes:
the Patriarchs, the Prophets, John the Baptist and Mary (the mother of
Jesus) and how these themes prepare the way for the coming of Jesus*
(2nd edition) (Glory to Glory Publications, 2014)
ISBN 978-0-9926674-2-9,
*Receive the Truth! – a collection of twenty questions and ten Bible talks
focusing on key issues in contemporary Christian-Jewish relations"* 2nd
edition (Glory to Glory Publications, 2011) ISBN 978-0-9567831-0-3

Morford, William
One New Man Bible – a fresh translation
ISBN 978-1-935769-11-8 (True Potential, Inc, 2011)
www,onenewmanbible.com

Pawson, David
By God, I Will – The Biblical Covenants
(Anchor Recordings, 2013) ISBN 978-0-9569376-8-1
Israel in the New Testament Extended edition
(Anchor Recordings, 2014) ISBN

Sammons, Peter
The Empty Promise of Godism – Reflections on the Multi-faith agenda
(Glory to Glory Publications, 2009) ISBN 978-0-9551790-6-8
Rebel Church – a challenge and an encouragement to the Believer
(Glory to Glory Publications, 2013) ISBN 978-0-9926674-0-5

Also from Glory to Glory Publications:

THE CASE FOR ENLARGEMENT THEOLOGY
Alex Jacob

A response to the impasse within contemporary Jewish-Christian relations, arising from the inherent weaknesses of replacement theology and two covenant theology in the light of Romans 9 – 11. Any mature Christian understanding of Jewish-Christian relations needs to make allowance for the theological background and history within which these relations have developed. Alex Jacob provides this background, as well as introducing a biblically faithful way between the two theological poles.

READY OR NOT – HE IS COMING
Stephanie Cottam

The Bible speaks of Jesus as the Bridegroom, and His followers as His Bride. The Day of His return for her will be a glorious day of rejoicing – but what exactly does all of this mean? What can we learn from the traditional Jewish wedding customs about "that glorious Day"? What does the relationship between a Jewish Bride and her groom tell us of our relationship with our Saviour, Jesus? And what does it mean for the Bride to have "prepared herself"? In *Ready or Not – He is Coming* Stephanie Cottam explores the biblical marriage rites in the light of Christian revelation and brings Jesus' simile to life in a straightforward and disarmingly simple way, but with a stark warning: Jesus was crystal clear that when He returns, not everyone will be ready for Him. Some will make their excuses and decline His invitation. Some of His watchmen will be asleep, spiritually speaking. A high proportion of foolish maidens will have no oil in their lamps – both groups will be left outside the wedding feast. What sort of a follower of Jesus are you? Are you prepared and ready – or half asleep, seeking other diversions during His long absence?

Also from Glory to Glory Publications:

PREPARE THE WAY
Alex Jacob

How does the birth and subsequent ministry of Jesus connect with the big picture of God's past promises and His future purposes? Alex Jacob explores this theme through the Church's traditional preparation for Christmas during its 'Advent' season – when it reflects on four key 'players' in the build up to the Messiah's birth: The Patriarchs, the Prophets, John the Baptist and Mary, the mother of Jesus. Each of these connects with the wider story of God's purposes.

This is not just a 'Christmas' book! The themes explored cover 2000 years of God's dealings with people up to the Birth of Jesus in Bethlehem, and look forward to His return in glory. Written in an accessible yet authoritative style, this is a helpful resource, suitable for private and group study. It sheds fresh light on God's faithfulness and on issues of our own personal discipleship. Foreword by Rev David M. Moore.

Alex Jacob is a United Reformed Church Minister, ordained in 1985. Since 2006, he has worked with The Church's Ministry Among Jewish People (CMJ). Alex has travelled and ministered widely in a teaching and leadership role and is also the author of two other books: *The Case for Enlargement Theology* and *Receive the Truth!* Both are published by Glory to Glory Publications.

THE BIBLE STUDENT

Fifty themed Bible studies aimed at helping people to understand God's purposes through the old and new testaments.

Inspired by and in a limited way, based on, the much loved and much reprinted *Every Man a Bible Student* (Joe Church, originally published by CMS in the 1930s) this is a brand new collection of studies, re-ordered and collected under generic theme headings.

The idea is simply to allow the Bible to speak on various subjects, using verses and passages that help to illustrate God's Mind as expressed in His Word. Wherever possible the studies move from the Old Testament to the New Testament and highlight the consistency between them.

There is undoubtedly a need for better Bible understanding among Christians and a similar need for clarity in exploring God's heart for those who are genuine seekers, whether Christian or not. This book helps to meet that need.

A handy help for all Christians who are serious in their discipleship. A useful gift to help those who are starting out on the Christian Way (e.g. the recently baptized, or those having been confirmed). A first point of reference to initiate deeper bible study.

All Christians must be "students" throughout their lives, learning at the feet of their Lord who so often is called "good teacher".

Edited by Peter Sammons, Director at Glory to Glory Publications, there are five key contributors. Their details are set out in the book.

Churches, individuals and mission organisations will all find a use for this helpful and inexpensive resource.